TOTALDESIGN

TOTALDESIGN

Contemplate, Cleanse, Clarify,
and Create Your Personal Spaces

clodagh

Text with Heather Ramsdell
Photographs by Daniel Aubry

Clarkson Potter/Publishers
New York

PHOTO CREDITS

DANIEL AUBRY: pages 10, 13, 18, 23, 24, 25, 26, 29, 30, 32, 33, 35, 36, 37, 38, 39, 40, 41, 43, 44, 45, 46, 47, 48, 49, 52, 53, 55, 56, 57, 58, 59, 60, 61, 62, 63, 65, 66, 67, 68, 69, 71, 73, 76, 77, 78, 79, 80, 81, 82, 83, 85, 86, 87, 88, 89, 90, 93, 96, 99, 101, 102, 111, 113, 114, 115, 116, 120, 121, 123, 124, 125, 126, 128, 134, 135, 136, 137, 138, 139, 140, 144, 148, 150, 151, 152, 154, 155, 159, 160, 161, 163, 164, 165, 168, 171, 173, 174, 175, 177, 179, 180, 181, 183, 186, 187, 188, 189, 191, 192, 193, 195, 196, 198, 200, 201, 202, and 203.

KEITH SCOTT MORTON: pages 18 (bottom), 21, 22, 23 (right), 26 (center), 27 (right two), 28, 29 (center), 30 (right, left), 48 (top), 49 (bottom), 64, 68 (lower right), 89 (lower left), 93 (upper right, lower right), 116 (center), 127, 129, 130, 132, 133, 138 (left, lower right), 140 (middle left), 147, 149, 156, and 163 (bottom).

LIZZIE HIMMEL: page 176.

Published by Clarkson Potter/Publishers, New York, New York. Member of the Crown Publishing Group.

Random House, Inc. New York, Toronto, London, Sydney, Auckland www.randomhouse.com

Clarkson N. Potter is a trademark and Potter and colophon are registered trademarks of Random House, Inc.

Printed in China

Design by Subtitle

Library of Congress Cataloging-in-Publication Data
Clodagh.
Total design : contemplate, cleanse, clarify, and create your personal spaces / by Clodagh.—1st ed.
Includes bibliographical references.
1. Interior design—Human factors.   2. Personal space—Psychological aspects.   I. Title.
NK2113.C625 2001
747—dc21
00-025174

ISBN 0-609-60519-4

10 9 8 7 6 5 4 3 2 1

First Edition

This book is my offering to you, the reader. My hope is that it serves to free your perceptions of the space around you.

ACKNOWLEDGMENTS

Those who have empowered me to create this book are many. My heartfelt gratitude goes to: My clients over the years; you made it all happen. My studio, my colleagues, and the hundreds of artisans, builders, and artists who shared in the creation of the projects. You have all brought a special gift of knowledge. My extraordinary partners: Robert Pierpont was there at the start; Steffani Aarons expanded our horizons; Ann Zieha, our studio director, sustained me with her wisdom, style, and passion for design. My husband, Daniel Aubry, whose photographs capture my work in images that linger in the mind. Pam Krauss, my editor, who came in search of the book I wanted to write, for her dry wit and pragmatism. Heather Ramsdell for sharing the words, and Marian Cohn, for carrying the torch for the final lap. Subtitle for sharing the vision. Jean Marie Parker, who edited the photography, understood the vision, and worked tirelessly to keep us on track. Fêng shui master Sarah Rossbach, who has brought harmony, balance, and prosperity to our projects and to our lives. Marjorie Lipari, my long-term astrological consultant. My friend and mentor, Jack Lenor Larsen, who once advised, "Don't take on a project unless you can make it wonderful!" My friend and honorary brother, Niall Smith, who is style personified. Karen Fisher, my design super agent. Mike Strohl and Chris Molinari, who have spread the good word. Kips Bay and DIFFA for showcasing my dreams. Ireland, which nurtured me, and all the countries I've visited for their inspiration. Spain for its generosity. My sons: Tim O'Kennedy, my marketing guru; Peter O'Kennedy, who composed the music for my installations; and Stephen O'Kennedy, who taught me so much in his brief lifetime; my grandchildren, Yan Bourke and Mia Bourke and their mother, Jackie Bourke; my stepdaughter, Valerie Aubry; Jay Heubert, her husband, and their children, Loren and Anna. And friends so many and so loving: Ilene Shaw, Beverly Russell, Margo Krasne, Tomio Nagaoka, Michael Claggett, and Nina Abrams, just to name a handful.

Contents

INTRODUCTION TO TOTAL DESIGN

12

If we were merely simple creatures, requiring nothing more from our homes than a shelter from the elements and a place to eat and sleep, we would be comfortable with very little: perhaps a room with a fire in one corner, a faucet in the other, and a mound of leaves to curl up on at night. As sentient, social, spiritual beings, however, we need rooms that allow us to think and to play, to reflect and to entertain friends, to bathe and to prepare meals. To truly support us, a home has to stretch beyond its material properties and sustain our complex human needs.

14

This book is about pleasure: discovering what pleases us and creating an environment that will celebrate those qualities and sustain us. Total Design is concerned with the *experience* of living and not simply the look of it. It is a healing art. It encourages an ongoing awareness of our surroundings to keep us energized and our shelters alive, not static.

A home cannot be truly beautiful unless it functions in harmony with who we are. Total Design is tough and sensual, utilitarian and spiritual. It considers all of our senses, our intellect and instincts, our spirit, and the health of our environment. It incorporates the principles of fêng shui, aromatherapy, color therapy, and astrology—but only to the degree that these philosophies nourish and mesh with your own guiding principles. There are no absolutes in Total Design;

no one approach works for everyone, and each of us needs different things from our environment. The goal of Total Design is both to help you discover what those needs are and to show you how to fulfill them with beauty and creativity for a uniquely personalized home. Beginning with who you are now and where you have been, Total Design clears a space for where you are going.

Begin by recognizing that everything about an environment affects you—the placement of walls, the flow of rooms, the quality of light, the texture of the floor beneath your feet. The rushed tempo of our lives lures us into following conventions that do not necessarily suit us. Carefully questioning these preconceptions creates an opportunity to celebrate many facets of life that have fallen by the wayside as casualties of routine. Just as new space appears from chaos when you rearrange a closet, a deep examination of the self, from your day-to-day routine to your most elusive dreams, clears space in your mind. You can literally make room for things that you have always wanted to do, such as exercise, paint, write, sculpt, meditate, or simply regroup and ground yourself. The simplest gesture can bring this about, and these gestures are the essence of Total Design. You will arrive at solutions that grow with you, enhancing your life without imposing on the natural environment we all must share.

Sources of inspiration are everywhere. We can learn from a daisy or a steel-belted radial. An old photograph or the sleeping quarters of a ship are equally inspiring. The constellation of influences that make their way into all of my projects includes the following: the search to make pleasure and meaning out of our senses, nostalgia, the physical size of a space, our relationship to nature, the ways in which we invent ourselves and the way others perceive us, our creature need for protection and retreat, the way we meet with nature in outdoor rooms and gardens, and the age-old search for a balance between body and spirit. And I always encourage finding new sources of inspiration.

Thinking this way does not always come naturally to us. Often, when we contemplate a space and how it can be improved we begin with the material (What kind of flooring do I want? Should I buy a new sofa or re-cover the old one?) rather than the spiritual (How can this room help me live better? What am I not getting from my home that I could be getting?) Inverting this kind of thinking is the starting point for embarking on Total Design.

...ISTS OF FOUR DISTINCT STAGES, MOST
... ANY PHYSICAL WORK ON THE SPACE
...THE FOUR C'S. IT STARTS WITH A DEEP
...OTH ME AND MY CLIENT UNDERSTAND
...TIMATELY DIRECTS HOW THE PROJECT
...A INTO FORM. BEFORE YOU EMBARK
...E REPURPOSING OF A SINGLE ROOM
...N EXISTING HOME—EVEN NEW CON-
...'ORK THROUGH THESE FOUR STEPS:
... CREATE.

...w does it make you feel and how do

...ng to move soon, let your experience

...you to identify sites of pleasure and sites of

...irritation. This information is completely reflective of your current

lifestyle, and it will help you find harmonious, life-enhancing solutions that will

free you to explore and change.

CLEANSE your life of unwanted and unused things. Two things nearly all of us could use more of are space and time. Clearing a pocket in space seems simultaneously to produce a clarity of thought that makes busyness more manageable and free time delightful. Clear out extraneous objects that are no longer useful or pleasing. It is harder to unload possessions than it is to acquire them, but emptiness lets a room grow and allows you to grow in it. Survey your closets, bookshelves, kitchen cabinets, and walls. Repair the broken objects that would still be useful to you. Auction off, sell, or give away the items that no longer make sense in your life. This task can seem overwhelming, and the help of a spouse or friend from the clutter-free school of thought can make it more manageable.

CLARIFY your goals, needs, and desires. This is the mental counterpart to clearing away physical clutter. What kinds of rooms and objects will really enhance your life? Which of your living habits are remnants of another time that no longer fit who you are now? Make sure you distinguish value from cost. A fountain may cost as much as a new suit but will continue to bring the outside in, offer soothing water music, humidify your space, and bring joy to your life for years after your suit has left for the thrift shop. Use the workbook that begins on page 209 to help you and those you live with identify the elements that are most important to you. Working through these exercises will help you

Opposite, top: The windows in this bedroom have been insulated from the sound of traffic for quiet contemplation. Overhead lights can be controlled from the entry or from remotes by the bed, which in accord with fêng shui has been placed auspiciously to have the best view of the windows.

Opposite, bottom: A trough of white orchids affords a sense of privacy in this limestone bathroom. Pivoting steel drawers provide ample storage. A ladder is draped with thick-piled bath towels; a mirrored trough with travertine stones deepens the perception of the room.

create a list that includes your necessities, your negotiable desires, and your dreams, and outline a budget.

CREATE. Having bushwhacked a path to your present self or selves, you can begin to create a space that is yours at its core.

Once you've worked through these stages, you'll have a far better sense of what you want from your home—and how to get it. Refer back to these four key words as the project evolves, noting any new thoughts that emerge along the way. Don't hesitate to revisit the first three steps as the project begins to take shape and as abstract notions become concrete.

A central precept of Total Design is that there are no givens. Our inherited notions of home layout can be confining. Total Design reconceives the elements of a home based on how they are used, regarding functional needs as an armature to build around.

It is very common for people to allow design to dictate what they do in a space, instead of using it to express who they are by serving their needs. I recently went to a consultation for a gigantic loft. Once I had seen all of the attractive and spacious common rooms, bedrooms, bathrooms, closets, and pantries, my hosts led me past a confusing dark area, far from any source of light. When my eyes adjusted to the dimness, I could barely make out, obscured behind a tower of boxes, a shapeless couch facing a television set. They sheepishly admitted that this room was where they spent most of their evenings. What they really enjoyed at the end of a long day was to relax together in front of the television set, but in their zealousness to spend more time reading, entertaining, and cooking, they realized they had shortchanged themselves on space to do this. We are multidimensional beings! The rooms of a home should respect all of our facets and not just the most optimistic ones.

Each room presents myriad opportunities for expressing who you are, what matters to you, and how you relate to the rest of the world. Too often we focus our creative impulses on the public spaces, allowing our personal sanctuaries to come together by default, an accumulation of castoffs or outgrown belongings. It is also common to neglect the spaces that have the greatest impact on those who enter. But even a small entryway or tiny outdoor space can make an important contribution to how you and others experience the dwelling.

Opposite: A sculptural coffee table harmonizes with an architectural chimney breast of burnished and raw steel. A slab of dusky plum slate anchors the hearth. Khaki artisan plaster walls flecked with grasses from the beach bring the outside in.

THE DOOR

The door is a sign. Its weight, the feel of the knob, the glide of the hinge, and the quality of its surface all convey a message about what awaits beyond. It is the drawbridge of a fortress, the curtain stretched across a stage, Alice's mirror into an alternate world. It can be a work of art in itself with a sculptural handle and forceful surface. Interior doors treated to match the walls virtually disappear when closed, turning the rooms behind them into secret chambers. In a small room, an unadorned door with a flush handle provides silence. Depending on how you treat it, the door can present an invitation or a dare.

Opposite: A tiny bulb hidden in a chandelier of stacked wire baskets sprays shadows within the vertical barrel vault of this polished plaster stairwell.

THE ENTRYWAY

Physically and psychologically, an entryway links the interior of a home to the outside world, welcoming us in and ushering us out again. Our experience there prepares the mind for what will follow.

A successful entryway will greet each of the physical senses. As in any transitional space, the impressions gathered in the few moments between the door and the interior are fleeting but powerful. The moment your toe crosses the threshold you inhale the aromatic signature of the space. Lace it with the quickening aroma of citrus or rosemary, the warm smells of wood and leather, the homeliness of sisal and beeswax. The visual focus of the experience can be a figure, such as a Buddha, a stand of flowers, an indoor fountain, or a work of art. Is the space

sound-absorbent or do you want an echo? Is there a smooth bench or chair to sit on for taking off shoes?

Once the door is shut and you are inside, you need to unload the bags, keys, mail, outer coats, and shoes that you brought home with you. Provide places near the door for these.

Don't forget that these spaces function both as entrance and exit. When you leave your home, what do your eyes rest on last? Applying the principles of the ancient Chinese art of placement, fêng shui, provides an aesthetic framework for where to locate paths and plantings or objects, and helps to establish balance and a flow of energy that lend solidity and harmony to the transition between indoors and outside.

23

THE KITCHEN

Le Corbusier said that a house is a machine for living. I agree, and I also apply this concept to office space, commercial space, hotels, and cars. The kitchen is a workplace, a studio, and an area of seduction. It is a room for communication and gathering. It is the first room most people go to after arriving home. Is there food? Yes, as well as water and a hearth. We can meet most of our creature needs without ever leaving the kitchen.

The beauty of a kitchen rises directly out of function. When it is designed around working with food, it will be a pleasure to spend time there. An attractive kitchen that is hard to work in is like a good-looking person with a bad personality. Even if your primary use of the room is preparing simple dinners of pasta and salad or unpacking take-out food and making coffee, having decent tools, ample work surfaces, and accessible storage space will make it an enjoyable place to be.

If cooking and entertaining are very important to you, your needs will be more specific. Celebrate them. Generosity is the key in work surfaces, light, ventilation, and storage. Build in enough storage for all of the utensils you now own, plus any that you think you will acquire in the next few years. Line the walls of a smaller kitchen with narrow shelving, about two glasses deep. An extra freezer or pantry for long-term storage is a practical addition that helps keep the space organized. Ample room for garbage and recycling should be worked into the design. Wherever possible, open the kitchen up with a counter or bar so that the cook can easily communicate with those in the common room or seating area.

The kitchen is the heart of the home, so design your kitchen to please yourself and to welcome friends and family.

Opposite: A splash of water from a stacked-glass fountain energizes steel and concrete in this urban kitchen.

THE DINING ROOM

My ideal dining room is a theater for feasting and wooing and for displaying cooking skills, taste, and an appreciation for whomever you're feeding, including yourself.

Begin with large, grounded shapes and spare decoration that will leave a lot of freedom for styling as your mood and the occasion demand. Leave enough space around the table so that when it is surrounded by people you can circle the room without bumping into chairs. Raising the dining area a few inches from the rest of the floor in an open space will separate it without secluding it. Finally, a low chandelier can hold the table in place and tint the room with twilight moodiness. Everyday meals can take place in the dining room: if you have one, enjoy it.

THE COMMON ROOM

The term "living room" implies that you don't live in the rest of the house. The common room is its own small civilization. It is the most public and often the largest area of the house, and it functions like an indoor courtyard where people meet to talk. The common room is the heart of a home, and as such, invites everyone, from strangers to intimate friends, to participate in the life of the home. It holds potential for every party that will take place there, for every piece of music to be played, and every conversation to be had. Like finding yourself alone in a gallery or a park, the experience of solitude in a place so vital and open has a special stolen quality.

Whichever activities you most value—entertaining guests, reading, playing chess, watching films, or listening to music—will determine the contents and the materials of the room. Television and sound equipment can be housed in built-in storage units behind doors so that when they are not in use they disappear, giving the room a more social mood. There should be one comfortable seat in this room for each member of the household.

THE MAIN BEDROOM

The bedroom should make pleasure and indulgence its focus—sleeping, lovemaking, lounging, reading. We spend about a quarter of our lives in bed, so fine bedclothes and a really good mattress are necessities that you should not deny yourself.

The more focused the bedroom is, the better. A separate erotic room is ideal, but not many people have enough space, so in every bedroom install a soft, low light on a dimmer switch. Increasingly, rooms are used for several distinct purposes, but certain functions do not mix well with sleep. Nothing is less conducive to romance or to sleep than a desk piled with bills, so place the office outside of the bedroom. Likewise, in a shared bedroom, an exercise

area may disturb the person who likes to sleep later. If there is space, dedicate a small room to clothing storage and dressing areas. If there isn't, you can separate them from the bed with a screen or partition.

What you see last before closing your eyes and see first upon waking should be pleasing to you. Position your bed to take advantage of any views through windows, or place an object that you love in your line of sight.

THE CHILDREN'S ROOMS

The single most important consideration when designing children's rooms is to provide the children with a place to ground themselves and explore and unfold in a safe and comfortable haven. Children who have been handed a room designed down to the last tieback are simply being handed their parents' notion of how their character is going to unfold. Give your children a safe environment in which they can grow and develop their own taste.

Opposite: A stainless steel tower conceals the showerhead and controls in this spacious bathroom, while visually slicing the shimmering glass. The vanity top is a single slab of cream-colored cast concrete.

THE BATHROOM

A cat or dog will pick a comfortable spot in a shaft of light to conduct its vital grooming. Human beings often groom themselves in the smallest, most uncomfortable room in the house. Wherever possible I separate the bathtub from the toilet, giving ample space and attention to the separate functions of grooming and eliminating waste.

Obviously bathing is the more social activity of the two, so in the tub room I install extra seating as well as reading lights, well-lit mirrors, and ample hooks for towels and robes. Like that from the bed, the view from the tub is fixed; make it pleasing by placing a white orchid nearby, or three pillar candles, a damp-proof piece of art, or a high window framing a square of sky.

THE PASSAGEWAYS

Hallways and stairways are spaces of transition. Because they are experienced in flux and not by a still eye, there is a lot of room for playfulness: the use of unusual materials, intense colors, intense artwork, especially absorbent or echoey materials to alter sound. In a home where the corridors are traversed several times a day, there should be enough details to keep you interested; tensile fabric tenting can endow the ceiling of a stairwell with light and shadow; portholes into other rooms, set high on hallway walls, create a puzzle of openings like a parlor game involving blindfolds; a hallway lined with shelves housing a library sets your mind in a contemplative space whenever you pass through it.

OUTDOOR ROOMS

Nature is healing. Bring the outside indoors, in the form of plants, light, and air, and let your interior flow outside into balconies and garden rooms. Whether you are working with a window box or acres of land, creating links between the outdoors and the interior of a place expands your sense of place in the world. Changes in foliage, walkway materials, and planting schemes signal the different functions of a series of garden rooms, which can include a meditation garden, a sunken garden, a dining garden, an aromatherapy garden. Incorporate play areas that can be trampled during riotous ball games. For houses without any outdoor property, window boxes both inside and outside can create the illusion of distance, like Japanese gardens mirroring entire landscapes in miniature.

DEDICATED ROOMS

Dedicated rooms are special areas designed around one particular activity that is central to your life and identity such as a game room, a dressing room, an exercise room, a project room, or a meditation room. Allow space for more than one such area if you can; they're a self-renewing indulgence. One client requested an art and style storeroom to store circulating artwork and tabletop items for entertaining. You may want to gather all of your books into a single book center furnished with a library table, chairs, and a table lamp or hanging light with a focused beam for reading. You might create a space where you can just sit and look at something you love.

Home offices, studios, and other work-oriented rooms may require special furniture or storage that does not fit with the general feel of a place. Give yourself an area in which to use your computer, handle incoming and outgoing communications, pay bills, and control the endless flood of papers that enter your life.

> It's only with the heart that one can see rightly.
> What is essential is invisible to the eye.
> —*Antoine de Saint-Exupéry*

As you read through the rest of the book, ideas may spring from the words or images. Keep a notebook at hand if you are planning changes in your living or your working space, and write down your first impressions. These are often the purest reflections of your feelings because they are uncensored by the intellect. The reasoning process can come later, together with budget and design negotiations with partner, spouse, or friend—or the toughest negotiation of all, with oneself. This is the beginning of your own contemplation process—the first step in applying the four C's to your own life and home. I've provided the Workbook at the end of this volume to guide you through the rest of the process.

It's lovely to hear "I love the color of my sofa," but Total Design goes much deeper than that. What I want to hear from clients after a project is complete is: "I love how my space feels." "My kitchen is a joy to work in." "My family communicates better." "My business is prospering." "We stay at home now because we love our space so much." "Our home is a haven." Then I know that my approach has worked.

In the chapters that follow, I've explored the primary themes that inform my design process as I work with clients to devise special spaces for them. You'll also encounter sections that take a closer look at the individual elements of Total Design, such as lighting, eroticism, windows, and welcoming guests. Finally, I offer a variety of color triggers to help you access your own deep-rooted connections to the infinite hues of nature and man's creations.

THE SENSES AND PHYSICAL SPACE

Sensory experience shapes the way you react to a space. As you move through any physical space, your eye is constantly scanning—for distance, color, light, size, the potential threat, the possible solace. You become aware of the temperature as you walk, as well as the air pressure, the vibrations, the weight and dimensions of the space. You register a spectrum of scents. Your ears filter meaning from sound.

Constantly and quietly, you categorize all this sensory information, automatically adding it to your internal library, the delicate database within that stores all memory, keeps you aligned, and regulates your moods and feelings.

Knowledge is not learning. Knowledge is experience.
—*Esteban Vicente*

Above: A versatile and lively sideboard by Wendell Castle is tucked into the sweeping curve of a plaster wall in this Manhattan maisonette, an example of art meeting function.

Opposite: Twin couches and a sculptural chair offer a welcoming perch from which to follow the afternoon sun. In the common room of the same Manhattan residence, the raised dining area is both a room and a stage.

Previous page: The simplicity of herringbone-patterned oak flooring and sculptured white walls draws attention to the art collection that fills this home. A ritual figure stands guard at the library door, while the carved rocker by Wendell Castle and a long table with blown-glass vases echo the architecture of a painting by Richard Diebenkorn and the playfulness of Alexander Calder's mobile. The ceiling is cut away for a rush of height. Flush baseboards minimize visual distraction so nothing interferes with the art.

When any sensory memory is triggered, it evokes a powerful idiosyncratic impression. Consider Proust and his madeleines or Napoleon and his violets. I call this the nostalgia of the senses. Consciously stimulating nostalgic experience that is happy and optimistic, serene and centered, is the linchpin of my design philosophy.

Modern life numbs the senses. Dashing from my Manhattan office to shop for dinner and then home, I find it hard to be mindful of the joy of living. Once in my apartment, however, the sound of water trickling against stones in my foyer carries me back to rushing streams in Ireland, to secret glades where I played as a child, to improvised fishing poles and a sense that my whole life stretched out before me.

I hear the water trickling and I remember that life is layered, that there is more to it than the frenzied pace of professional demands. I tap into another mode of being. I breathe deeply. All of this happens without my thinking about it. A single sound changes me. And life goes on.

Each of the human senses can stimulate nostalgia. It could be a visual image, a scent, or the feel of the doorknob that returns you to yourself when you enter your home. Total Design considers them all and creates spaces that engage various senses at various times. Total Design means gaining a fuller awareness of your particular responses to qualities of light, color, shape, texture, and scent.

Sight is probably the first sense to consider; it is certainly the most readily described. It is easy to recognize that something is, for instance, yellow and big and far away. And it is equally easy to agree on these perceptions. While it may exist in different shades and hues, yellow is yellow. In addition, there is a consensus that yellow is good, yellow is cheerful, yellow is warm. We call the sun yellow. Yet everyone has intimate, personal associations with the color yellow. Only by becoming aware of a particular client's feelings for yellow can I maximize the effect of that color in my design.

The writer Susan Sontag claims that sight is the most promiscuous of the senses, hungrily touching as much as it can at all times. Even so, the human eye sees by degrees. So visual design works by degrees, from the largest sweeping view to the smallest captivating detail. To fully engage the eye, a design moves, as does the sight line, from the universal to the highly specific.

Scent, on the other hand, is as subtle and difficult as sight is immediate. Per-

haps this is because smell is the least social of all our senses. Indeed, in modern culture, smell is slightly suspect, with an entire industry devoted to obliterating human odor and the organic progression of life from ripe to rotten. In this context, society seems to have agreed that neutral is safe.

Incorporating aroma into design is a dangerous business. But scent is too potent and bewitching an element to ignore. A single whiff can transport you back to the first time you experienced a smell. Lavender and thyme might carry you to the south of France; balsam might take you back to the woods of your childhood; the smell of baking apples might carry you back to an idealized home, to one perfect moment. Smell can also identify a person—if you miss your lover, you open his closet and inhale.

Like the sense of smell, touch is more intimate than social. Hearing, on the other hand, like seeing, is easy to describe and simpler to agree upon. As intimate as the associations individuals may have to what they see or hear, there is a large common ground, a nearly universal range of pleasant stimuli. Whether incorporating elements for sight or sound, or for the more intimate senses of smell and touch, a finely honed balance is essential. We humans, however, routinely push the senses beyond biological usefulness, solely for pleasure. Sex, for instance, calls upon all the senses at once, and invents others along the way. Yet experience shows that abuse of pleasure robs us of its intended effect. Pleasure without meaning is empty.

The need for meaning distinguishes human beings from other creatures. The most powerful sensory provocation is one that resonates with memory, purpose, and meaning. Surrounding yourself with meaningful objects and materials engages you more fully in the present, because it is a pleasure to be there. Living your life in this way is not unlike looking at a painting or carefully listening to a piece of music: you tune your awareness to a deeper world operating beneath the surface. You are more aware of simply breathing, moving, and being in time and space. In Total Design, spaces are customized canvases. The lives lived in these canvases are art.

The Chinese practice of fêng shui has long studied the relationship between energy and people and their spaces. It is an essential element of my designs, as it helps me determine how to place objects so that the space beckons for reasons that are not immediately understood. Allow enough space so that each object can breathe and provide enough comfort so that people will linger. It is

Above: Knife slots carved directly into the counter are well out of the reach of children but easily accessible by the cook.

Opposite: In this cherry-wood and stainless-steel kitchen, a square of butcher block provides an inviting place for an informal lunch for four. The stove has been placed in a protected area in accord with fêng shui to allow the cook to see what is going on.

overwhelming to have all the elements vying for attention at once, so sight lines must be directed. Fêng shui helps me to design spaces that are compassionate and serene but also enlivening.

Designing a living space well means celebrating all the senses and the intellect. You also want your living space to tempt and tantalize and challenge you to fully enjoy its sensuality. The ordinary objects of a house can also gently encourage us to reflect—the surface of a wall, a sturdy column, the heft of a glass of cool, clean water as you raise it to your lips. Nothing should be taken for granted. If a design is too predictable, it will lull your senses. A bathtub in the bedroom keeps you on your toes, though I don't ever place elements solely to shock— no toilet in the common room, for example. The tub has to be there for a valid reason, such as the enjoyment of talking to your lover while she soaks. A living space is like a life partner—it supports the total person, not simply one or two facets of the personality. It should be forgiving and kind.

Emptiness invites activity. I account for future play and development by building in emptiness in the form of tables, vases, bowls, and hooks. Finishing a place down to the type of napkin allowed on the table is too limiting. When you keep the variables simple, the options open up. A carved wooden bowl in the kitchen can be filled in July with peaches or tomatoes bursting with juices in August. In October it will be heaped with apples that fill the kitchen with the last deep sweetness of summer.

A beautiful bowl that rings sonorously when you put your keys in it gives pleasure each time you pass through the door. Lining the stairs with a lively kilim rug makes mounting them seem like an exotic journey. A sculptural lamp that casts a calming yellow light is evocative of Japanese garden lanterns in summer. A corner of a groin vault or the shadows of a ziggurat are deeply affecting, though, like most people, I can't easily describe why these shapes and shadows are so moving. These touches rouse your senses and remind you to pay attention and stay awake and to respect the physical life around you.

When I contemplate a new project, what is most important to me is that the life lived in that space is enhanced. Visual art, music, literature, and fine food enjoy a place of privilege in our hearts and minds, representing the apex of human achievement.

Top: The mold for this cast-bronze fireplace and mirror frame was sculpted on-site.

Above: A curve of glowing resin, banded with raw steel, provides texture and light in a library.

Opposite: Plush fabrics, African-inspired ebony tables, the warmth of wood, and a collection of books invite intimacy and introspection.

Breathing Room

WALLS GIVE A HOUSE STRUCTURE AND DEFINITION, BUT THEY ACHIEVE THIS IN MYRIAD WAYS. IT IS POSSI-BLE TO DEFINE A SPACE WITHOUT CONFINING IT, SUCH AS THE USE OF SUBTLE DESIGN CUES THAT SUB-CONSCIOUSLY DRAW YOU INTO AN AREA AND TELL YOU WHAT YOU SHOULD BE DOING THERE. HERE ARE A FEW IDEAS THAT I FIND WORK ESPECIALLY WELL:

SURFACES

- Changes of color, pattern, and material used in walls and floors psychologically establish boundaries between areas.
- When dividing a larger room into different areas, it is important that the room retain a sense of whole-ness. Keep the cues subtle and work within the existing palette of colors. Introduce a different pat-tern in each area, or change the color of one wall by a few shades or a few hues.

DROPPED CEILINGS AND RAISED FLOORS

- A low archway in an entry hall invites traffic to flow into the farther, taller room.
- Dropping a ceiling above close seating creates a warm nest within a larger room.
- A platform makes a stage for a thronelike bed or a dining room table.

FURNITURE PLACEMENT

- Nestling a couch or a desk in a corner creates a feel-ing of security and comfort because no one can come up behind you.
- A substantial table grounds a dining area. A vault or low chandelier over the table fixes it emotionally at the center of the pool of light.
- Seating areas should be arranged around a well-defined view, be it of the backyard garden or the common room hearth.

VERTICAL DIVISIONS

- Columns, pillars, and partial walls are often struc-turally necessary, but they are also psychologically

effective ways of opening up rooms while defining room perimeters. A row of columns can outline a common room.
- An open kitchen allows the cook to be involved with conversation on the other side of the counter, while keeping the kitchen clear of extra bodies. Outward-facing counters, a carefully positioned rolling cart, or freestanding corners achieve this.
- A colonnade of tall plants or a heavy wooden or metal screen will create a physical barrier while allowing guests to peek into the protected room.

PARTIAL WALLS

- A frosted glass wall creates a pocket of visual pri-vacy while allowing light to be shared.
- Walls that don't reach the ceiling let heat and air and sound flow above them while keeping the person behind them visually protected.
- A slot in a large wall is a playful and elegant way to connect rooms.

TEMPORARY WALLS

- A deep window seat with louvered doors creates a tiny private reading room or perfect place for napping.
- Rolling storage screens can house books or collec-tions, and can be rolled flat against a wall when you need more floor space. They can create visual pri-vacy for an overnight guest, or spare you from the guilty reminder of your work space.
- Pocket doors can roll out to make an instant guest room, or to shield private areas of the house from guests.

SENSUAL TEXTUR

ES

Patinated steel and distressed leather;
interlocking bronze plates, rustic, sun-
baked terra-cotta tiles from Mexico;
tumbled travertine tiles; river stones and
poured concrete.

Art Handling

CAREFUL HANGING OF VISUAL ART ENHANCES AND CELEBRATES BOTH THE ART AND THE SPACE IN WHICH IT'S HOUSED. IN A RESIDENTIAL SETTING IT REQUIRES SPECIAL ATTENTION BECAUSE PEOPLE NOT ONLY STAND BEFORE THE ART; THEY ALSO SIT, LIE DOWN, AND WALK PAST IT ON A DAILY BASIS. THERE ARE NO HARD AND FAST RULES FOR DISPLAYING ART, BUT IT IS HELPFUL TO KNOW ABOUT CERTAIN TRADITIONS. YOU MAY FIND THAT AN INDIVIDUAL PIECE WILL CLUE YOU IN TO WHAT IT WANTS FOR ITSELF. TRY A PIECE IN SEVERAL SETTINGS TO FIND THE BEST PLACE FOR IT.

HANGING PAINTINGS

- Centering and leveling a painting sets it solidly on a wall so that you can concentrate on the art, not its disorienting relationship to nearby corners or the ceiling.
- A family of art hung together will read as a single story—for better or worse. Some pieces suffer when forced to compete with others, while others are enriched by clustered salon hanging or group placement.
- Delicate watercolors and small or light drawings need to be placed where you can step up close to them.

THREE DIMENSIONS

- If a room does not allow a sculpture or figure to be placed so that you can walk around it, an architectural mirror behind the piece will enable you to view it in all its dimensions.
- You can direct light at a sculpture from unpredictable directions and make conscious use of the shadows it casts.
- Elevating a small sculpture on a platform or in a niche set into the wall brings it closer to eye level and human scale.

BACKGROUND

- A neutral backdrop usually offers the most desirable setting in which to view art. White walls provide one kind of neutrality, but color often vibrates too strongly against white. Natural beiges and grays provide a softer context for viewing.
- Vivid paintings can take on the eloquence of stained glass if hung on walls of the right color. Taupe, parchment, paper-bag brown, or, surprisingly, red can reinforce strong pieces.
- Wallpaper with graphic patterns will compete unpleasantly with most paintings, but sculpture can work in such a space.

CARE

- Direct sunlight can have as bad an effect on your art as it does on your skin, so use sun-blocking shades and filters on windows.
- Be careful of humidity, especially in bathrooms, and of grease buildup near kitchens.
- Place fragile objects out of reach or in a case.
- If you need to store a piece of art, use archival storage materials—most commercial glues and cardboards contain acids or damaging chemicals.
- If your art has financial and artistic value, make sure it is properly protected, framed, or covered, and have it authenticated for insurance purposes.

ROTATING

- Even a masterpiece can become wallpaper if the eye becomes too accustomed to it. Some people like to keep a curatorial closet so that they can rotate their art when it begins to weaken with familiarity.
- Installing a simple rail or hanging system means that you can move art around without putting new holes in your walls.
- Art can also be firmly integrated into the architecture of a place in permanent niches or sconces. These works are like family members that live and change in meaning along with you.

ART YOU LIVE WITH

- The selection of art is as personal and revealing as your choice of clothing. If an artwork is unpleasant to one of the people living in your home, place it in a less central corridor or in the study of the person who does like it.
- One of the goals of art may be to rouse and disturb, but there is no reason to live with art you don't like. Critics can point out an artwork's cultural importance, quality of craft, or importance in history. If you like the work this information will help you to appreciate it more, but if you don't like it, these assessments won't make it easier to live with.

MATCHING THE ART TO THE ROOM

- Art appeals to people in a very visceral way.
- I place provocative or unsettling art in walk-by or gallery areas. Harmonious, quiet art hangs in bedrooms.
- A common room or dining room can support exciting, stimulating artworks.
- Portraits are like watchmen or friends and can be placed wherever their company will be most appreciated.
- Food-related art will look great in the kitchen.
- Prop recent and favorite photos on ledges, where you can constantly rearrange and update them.
- Masks and other three-dimensional artworks look great when hung in an unpredictable location, such as above a doorway or in a corner of a passageway.

WHITE

JET TRAILS ABOVE A HUGE DUVET OF CLOUDS. THE HEAVY
TRANSLUCENT STICKY RICE. A LINE OF APPLE TREES IN BLOOM
MOONLIT SWIMMER. A COOL SLIVER OF MOON ABOVE THE
TION OF THE PARTHENON IN THE MORNING. THE LUMINOUS
GRIN THROUGH THE TOKYO MIST. THE FLAMENCO FRILL OF
THROUGH THE ARCHES OF A LIME-WASHED COURTYARD
SOMS AT TWILIGHT. MOURNING IN THE EAST AND WEDDINGS
JUNE MORNING BREEZE. A SHAFT OF SUNLIGHT ON A SHEET
TION OF TILES. A FLOTILLA OF YACHTS IN RHODE ISLAND. A
MERINGUES. COCONUT MILK, AND MILK OF ALL KINDS. A SLOW
THE EXPECTANT STARE OF UNPAINTED CANVAS AND BLANK
ING INTO A NOVEMBER SKY. THE WHITE OF AN EYE. THE FLAG
OVER THE HEDGE. EASTER VOTIVES FLICKERING IN A MUSTY

WHITE OF A POLAR BEAR IN AN EPHEMERA OF SNOW.
PHOSPHORESCENCE DRIPPING FROM THE FINGERS OF A
LACEWORK OF THE TAJ MAHAL. THE ANCIENT WHITE SEDUC-
FACE OF A GEISHA. THE PEAK OF MOUNT FUJI FLASHING A
SURF ON THE SPANISH COAST. A STALLION RUSHING
TCHAIKOVSKY'S "WALTZ OF THE FLOWERS." MAGNOLIA BLOS-
N THE WEST. A DRIFT OF CLEAN WINDOW CURTAINS ON A
FLAPPING AGAINST THE GREEN GRASS. A GRIDDED PERFEC-
TUCKED-IN CONVENT BED. WONDER BREAD, MARSHMALLOWS,
PROCESSION DOWN THE AISLE TOWARD THE BRIDEGROOM.
PAPER. INFINITY. SWANS ON BLACK WATER. DOVES SCATTER-
OF SURRENDER. THE SALT OF ÎLE DE RÉ. HAWTHORN FOAMING
CHURCH. THE MATTE SILENCE OF A LONG PLASTERED HALL.

PURE LIGHT

THE POWER
OF NOSTALGIA

As the path from birth to the end of our lives proceeds in zigzags and curves and circuits, we can revisit and reinterpret sites from the past with a wiser eye. The successes and pleasures of where we have been coalesce with the present to make a life that grows increasingly meaningful and resonant and full with its own particularity. Each of us possesses a storehouse of mental artifacts. We can sift what is best from them to build a shelter that reflects us in our own best light.

Every room is a living room.

A home is a reflection of the mind. It is endlessly faceted, filled with history and possibility, coalesced into a singular whole. I am always struck by the mind's wonderful ability to cleanse itself. It spares us from much of the painful, boring, or defunct material of life by blurring, erasing, and pushing many details into deep storage. Yet we still have access to scenes and vignettes from the past and can replay them, like tapes, at will. Often the tiniest sliver of an experience is all that will stay with you. The special glint of a burnished chair's arm rather than an entire sitting room.

My childhood comes to mind. I recall walking into the dining room of our house in Ireland one day when the sun was streaming through the window onto a pile of sweet peas. My mother was sitting in a chair, backlit, and though I can't see her face in this memory, I remember the richness and warmth of her voice, the fragrance of the peas on the table, and the smell of Johnson's lavender wax. That moment has clung fast for all these years, while entire months of routine have been smudged out of memory.

It is the kindness of nostalgia that allows us to retrieve these pieces of our past when it suits us to do so. And as I sit with clients discussing how their rooms will take shape, I love to pluck aspects from their past that can be incorporated as positive forces in the new environment.

The elusiveness of memory took especially satisfying form in one project in New York City. The owners of this 7,000-square-foot penthouse had traveled the world extensively, and influences from all their travels enter into the design: the color and texture of Tuscany, massive, slightly canted columns from Egypt, Tibetan figures of Buddha alongside the steel kitchen equipment of professional restaurants. Diverse sources fold together naturally in every corner of the space because these elements spring from experiences in the clients' lives. The environment is fresh and entirely specific to them. When we couldn't find something ready-made, we had it built—over fifty artisans, plaster workers, metalworkers, artists, and cabinetmakers worked on this project.

The building was still under construction when we began planning the design, and the penthouse was a slab of concrete twenty-seven stories above the street. We had already tossed away limiting preconceptions about living space—that a bedroom must have two nightstands, for example, or that a dining room should be reserved for special occasions. And, as we always do, we started with questions: Where have you been happiest? How do you actually

56

Above: The study and TV room share the fireplace and a terrace view.

Opposite: Massive canted columns frame this view to the living room.

Previous page: An offset skylight simultaneously mixes light and volume to create mystery. The vault is plastered in muted shades that give way into a gray-blue as it extends up toward the sky. During the day, sunlight is reflected without glare. Out of view, a light is set back so that at night it seems as though moonlight is shining down.

(continued on page 62)

Influence

BORROWING FURNISHINGS AND TRADITIONS FROM
OTHER TIMES AND CULTURES HAS ALWAYS BEEN
PART OF HOME DESIGN—THE WORLD IS RICH WITH
THESE SOURCES. BUT INSPIRATION CAN ALSO BE
FOUND IN NONDOMESTIC REALMS SUCH AS WORK
SPACES, PUBLIC SPACES, NATURAL SPACES, AND LIT-
ERARY SPACES, AND THEIR PURPOSE, COLOR, TEX-
TURE, AND MATERIAL CAN BE USED TO FOCUS THE
GENERAL IMPACT OF A DESIGN. CONSIDER THE
FOLLOWING:

- The workshop aesthetic of an artist's studio
- The shiny functionality of the inventor's lab
- The mute solidity of a beach cave
- The clean, heavy-duty industrial kitchen
- The lofty simplicity of a temple
- The warm roughness of a barn
- The silent orderliness of a library
- The freshness of a grade school

Each room within a house can suggest a different kind
of space. Where do you enjoy spending time? Make
those places part of your daily life.
- The closet is a boutique.
- The kitchen is a restaurant.
- The common room is a piazza.
- The bedrooms are monastery cloisters.
- The dining room is a banquet hall.
- The corridor is a city street.
- The stairwell is a secret passageway.
- The bathroom is a running stream.
- The meditation room is a mountain cave.
- The children's room is a playground or a studio.
- The storage room is a market.

The suggestion need not be extravagant; one carefully
chosen object can gesture to worlds outside of home
life without disturbing a more traditional domestic
environment. These elements send strong messages:
- Stainless steel carts
- Industrial kitchen equipment
- Unfinished wooden joists on the ceiling
- Store display racks in closets for shoes and clothing
- Checkerboard linoleum floors
- Poured concrete surfaces
- A celestial bed from a nineteenth-century novel
- Thick spa-grade towels and linens
- High windows that filter in light but reveal only
  the sky

My deep respect and love for great art inspires me to try to incorporate aspects of it into my design. I'll often find a fragment that expresses something so perfectly that it will form the basis for a whole habitat. The colors of this door were inspired by a corner of an Anselm Kiefer painting I saw at the Museum of Modern Art in New York.

A slot cut into the wall behind the Buddha was filled with sandblasted glass. A dim spot illuminates the back of the glass to allow the wall to become a glowing light. A thick wedge of wall hides two sliding doors to close off a versatile room.

Above: The kitchen, situated at the heart of the home, boasts a salamander, a wood-burning pizza oven, and a large, temperature-controlled wine room. Although it is 18 feet away from the nearest window, the counter is flooded with daylight from a slotted skylight.

Opposite: The dining room is designed as a blank stage set. Grounded by a massive 6-foot-square table made of alcove stone set on a patinated steel base, the natural linen chairs wheel into various seating arrangements. A round mirror brings in good views along with chi and fulfills Sarah Rossbach's request to "bring in the city" for the diners seated with their backs to the window.

(continued from page 56)

spend your time at home? In what ways did your past homes fall short?

It soon became evident that a very significant source of shared nostalgia for this couple was Tuscany, where for many summers they had rented a farmhouse. There the long afternoons were spent on terraces where they gathered around a long, wooden table to eat and talk. We re-created this feeling with a massive stone table and a long concrete kitchen counter where everyone could congregate. Stocks of vinegar, wine, oil, and the aroma of spices fill the kitchen, recalling long mornings spent shopping in bountiful markets, and afternoons spent preparing and eating food, laughing, and telling stories.

Designing around personal nostalgia is most effective when the space remains flexible to a variety of temporary styling elements. If the nostalgia is too specific, it grows invisible. We kept the dining room spare so that on one day it might be decked out for a Tuscan dinner with lavish terra-cotta bowls and plates and a feast of Mediterranean ingredients, while at another time it could host a minimal dinner of noodles in lacquer bowls. For their daughter's wedding party, a high-rise cake and froth of cherry blossoms filled the foreground of the extraordinary twenty-seventh-floor view.

Their living room is also uncluttered. The plaster walls are satiny and strokable, the floors are color-washed wood. A minimal living room will never be identical to a summer in Tuscany, but a room honed down to essentials re-creates a pocket of the clarity these people experienced there.

Just as memory can serve to inspire design, so too can the objects we encounter in the world around us. For us, a trip to the Metropolitan Museum of Art in search of color inspiration was serendipitous. Instead of the elusive shade of blue we sought, we were all struck by the massiveness of the canted columns in the Egyptian wing. As is true with every penthouse, all of the functions of the building ran up through the center of the space: the elevator, air conditioning vents, and lightning conductors. We wondered how we could make the problem into an opportunity. By utilizing the massive tilted column of Egyptian architecture, we grounded the lofty space architecturally while con-

Migratory Eating

THERE'S SOMETHING EXTREMELY GRATIFYING ABOUT EATING IN A VARIETY OF SPOTS AROUND THE HOUSE. MAYBE THE CHANGE SIMPLY KEEPS YOU ALERT TO WHAT YOU ARE TASTING. THE REASONS DON'T REALLY MATTER. CERTAIN FOODS SIMPLY LOVE CERTAIN PLACES. POPCORN IS TRANS- FORMED BY THE BLUE FLICKER OF A MOVIE IN THE DARK. TO CONSUME A BOWL OF CHERRIES IN A WHITE BED IS SENSUALITY ITSELF TINGED WITH A SENSE OF DANGER. NEWSPAPERS AND COFFEE ARE INFINITELY BETTER ON A TALL STOOL AT A BREAK- FAST BAR. WHATEVER ROOMS DRAW YOU TO EAT IN THEM, SET UP A PLACE THERE FOR YOURSELF: BRUNCH AT A SMALL TABLE NEAR A SUNNY WIN- DOW; A RAINY SUNDAY LUNCH ON A LOW STOOL AT THE COFFEE TABLE; A DECADENT FRIDAY NIGHT TAKE-OUT DINNER IN FRONT OF THE TV; ANY MEAL AT ANY TIME AT A TABLE IN THE OPEN AIR; AND ON THE COUCH A LARGE TRAY OF TEA AND COOKIES AND FRUITS. ONE OF LIFE'S GREATEST LUXURIES IS EATING IN BED.

64

cealing a great deal. The column also contains storage space for kitchen tools.

To further surround the owners with affirming memories, we created a long, angular gallery in the hallway in which to display various pieces collected during their travels—Buddhas from Thailand, elephants from India, a lush Botero painting of a fat hunter reflected in a pool of water. The hall culminates in a fireplace that acts as a beacon toward the warmth of the hearth.

Reconnecting with one's own personal nostalgia is essential to Total Design. It is also a richly rewarding adventure into sense memory, a hunt for the buried treasures of life's experience, the moments and places that have resonated most profoundly with one's deepest sense of self. The discovery begins with a simple self inquiry: *Where have I felt the happiest in my life?*

You may find this easier to do with a confidant or partner primed to ask the questions and jot down notes. A glass of good wine each, a quiet space, and an allocated time slot of at least ninety minutes will help to prompt the friendly delving that can jump-start the process.

As images surface, remember the place, the season, the time of day—specific moments of happiness, if you can. Is the site of your nostalgia a château or a cottage? A kitchen or a bedroom? Do you envision a massive four-poster bed with a chaise on either side, or rag rugs on stone floors and drifts of Irish linen? Book-lined walls with tall French windows opened to a garden, or whitewashed Grecian rooms, minimal and luminous against a startling blue sea?

In your mind's eye, survey the surroundings. Walk from room to room; explore the landscape. Are you alone? Is there conversation? A particular activity? Revisit the experience with each of your senses. What is the scent of the Adriatic? The sound and color of the breaking waves? The texture and temperature of a fistful of sand? Can you still see the particular glint of sunlight through a window? Examine every remembered mood or image as you might a found object at an archaeological dig, gently dusting off layers of forgotten time, question by question, until all the pleasurable details are revealed.

Family photos and old home videos can help jog the imagination. They are

Above: Antique spoons made from animal horn serve as door handles for a linen closet stenciled with the geometry of West-African mud cloth.

Opposite: The room colors of slumbering lion and dried grass were inspired by a recent trip to Africa. The tall screen is reminiscent of Masai shields leaning against a hut. The room encourages gathering with family or quiet solitude. A high-backed sofa is ready for a long conversation with a friend. The oversize chair with ottoman is called "the Edith Chair" in honor of beloved Edith Wharton. The wool rug is an abstraction of layered animal skins. Soft down pillows are ready to accommodate a snooze by the fire. A wall niche holds a collection of books for easy reference or casual browsing.

A friendly Buddha welcomes visitors to this home; in a Japanese-inspired bathing pavilion, light slices through the slats of a recycled lumber ceiling. A cast-concrete tub sits on a limestone slab, while the oversize wall sconce creates a window of light. The scent of jasmine wafts from aromatherapy candles. Steel bud vases are reminiscent of bamboo.

often excellent if inadvertent catalogs of a lifetime of personal artifacts—the particular fabric of a once-favorite dress, the collection of objects atop a parent's dresser, holiday chatter around Grandmother's oak table. Recorded sights and sounds of childhood shake loose lost memories of once-familiar things that still evoke feelings of love, comfort, and joy.

Look around you in the present moment, too. What have you gathered to your home from recent travels? An African mask, spices from Sri Lanka, Buddhas from Bangkok? Focus on the artifact and remember the feeling of being there. If photographs are important to you, find an image of the place itself captured by a great photographer. Even in black and white, a picture of the Grand Canyon can conjure up technicolor memories of clay red, turquoise blue, and adobe, and reinspire a love affair with southwestern terrain or native American forms and designs. An old postcard of the beach at Biarritz may bring to mind a winter's stay at a grand hotel. You may never be able to re-create the palatial *salle de bain* of your memory, but you can capture elements of its design that will recall the timeless luxury of the place and evoke its special charm: the classic shape of porcelain faucets, the warmth of a rosewater bath and thick heated towels, floor-to-ceiling windows, the delight of morning sun filtered through white voile and reflected in a vanity mirror.

Sometimes the sight of familiar things will have the opposite effect, blurring, rather than spurring, memory and numbing feeling. Then it is time for a change of scenery. Take a long car trip anywhere or a brief busman's holiday at a local museum. Either way, bring a journal and notice where you are drawn to go. Did you drive to the mountains or the shore? City or country? Did you window shop or eat? Read or listen to music? At the museum, did you linger in the Egyptian wing or at the pre-Columbian art? At Giacometti or Rodin? John Singer Sargent or Jasper Johns? Make notes as guidelines for the moment of decision.

Personal nostalgia is truth and experience. It is impossible to edit. It brands your senses and will not fail you. Rely on it like a good friend when you are creating your space.

Opposite: A sensuous and curvaceous armchair with a graphite leather seat is formed from satin-charcoal patinated steel. For good fêng shui, a row of step lights rims this small room.

Let There Be Light

LIGHT IS LIFE. LIGHT GIVES ENERGY. LIGHT IS ESSENTIAL TO OUR WELL-BEING. LIGHT CAN CHANGE A MOOD FASTER THAN ALMOST ANY OTHER DESIGN TOOL. BAD LIGHTING CAN DEADEN A GOOD DESIGN.

KINDS OF LIGHT There are many kinds of light, both in nature and in the environments we frequent, each of which can trigger specific feelings of well-being or pleasurable nostalgia:

- Streaks of light and shadow while driving through a dense wood on a brilliant day
- The rosy light of predawn
- The dazzling white of ski slopes
- Focused circles of light in the dark, swirled with the smoke of incense and filled with the sound of clinking glasses
- Fresh first autumn daylight
- Mysterious jagged light from a bonfire
- The silkiness of a skylight on a slightly hazy day
- Cool blue moonlight

Think about the kinds of light that invigorate or calm you, and re-create them using natural light from windows and skylights as well as colored shades, candles, and various kinds of bulbs.

Halogen, incandescent, fluorescent. The range of wavelengths shed by different types of bulbs can dramatically alter the mood of a room. Using them in combination will give you a great range of options for creating various moods and occasions. *Halogen bulbs* cast a very white light and take up a minimum amount of space, making the fixtures less conspicuous. They are also quite hot. Yellow *incandescent light* is lively and warm. The shadows are sharp. They cast a sheen on people's hair and eyes. Many types of *fluorescent lights* have a flattening effect, making skin, hair, and eyes look washed out and dulling materials like wood and glass, which should be lustrous and deep. They are inexpensive but they can bring down the energy level of a room. Color-corrected fluorescent lights include a wider spectrum of color that is more flattering and upbeat than regular fluorescents, yet still cool and cost-efficient. *Daylight* is stimulating because it is constantly changing as clouds and mists pass over the sun. Lighting with shadows simulates this excitement. Divide your lighting into three types:

Focused task lights light your book or documents, your work surface, or your face for applying makeup or shaving.

Hidden lights and gallery lights direct attention toward the objects they illuminate: a painting, a sculpture, or a photo wall.

Ambient light illuminates the air of a space and captures light in forms.

The most successful spaces combine various kinds of light. For kitchens, most people prefer a combination of spotlighting for work areas, and ambient lighting to diffuse the shadows of objects. The combination is clean-looking and easy to work in. In a bedroom, ambient light emanating from a source close to the floor is calming, and lamps create pockets of brightness in which you can read or groom yourself. Hidden lights impart a stately solidity for transitional spaces such as halls and stairways.

OCCASION LIGHTS Each bedroom should contain a low, dim light operated on a switch. Architectural outdoor lamps flood a space with light and can create the excitement of daytime on the darkest night when they shine through a skylight. Sculptural lamps can stand on their own as objects whether or not they are lit. The functionality of any closet is increased by even a simple incandescent bulb set into the wall.

THE DARK Mastering light means understanding its counterpart, dark. Darkness is the visual equivalent of silence. Shadows are the bonus of light, creating graphic kinetic patterns in places that might otherwise be static. Place small spotlights beneath plants to throw vibrant organic dappling on the ceiling. Notice the patterns your windows make. A cluttered windowsill throws a cluttered shadow. Geometric panes or blinds, glass bottles of different shapes, or a single sun-loving plant will trace the passage of time across your wall.

OFF AND ON Put your lights on dimmers to get a wider range of lighting options from the same fixtures; dim lights for night parties, bright lights to wake you on a dark February day. Place switches at the entrances of rooms and at both the top and bottom of staircases. Adding an extra switch or remote system near the bed is a luxury as indispensable as a remote control.

YELLOW

A FIELD OF WHEAT STRIATED BY CLOUD SHADOWS. THE SEDUC
FUME OF GORSE. CASCADES OF LABURNUM BLOSSOMS IN A
THE FLASH OF AN AVAILABLE YELLOW CAB ON A WET MORNING
SUMMER EVENINGS. THE PURE HALO OF BIRCH TREES IN THE

TIVE ACIDIC PROMISE OF PILES OF LEMONS. THE WARM PER-
JUNE GARDEN. THE SENSUAL BEAT OF A BRAZILIAN SAMBA.
THE OCHER WALLS OF TUSCANY. THE LONG GOLDEN LIGHT OF
FALL. THE GOLD OF A RENAISSANCE TRIPTYCH.

SIZE COUNTS: SMALL SPACES

A feeling of spaciousness is determined far more by clarity and energy flow than by square feet. Any small space should be a luxury of clarity and paring down. The key resides in skillful editing and finding the essence of your particular needs.

I have made this letter longer than usual because I lack the time to make it short.
—Blaise Pascal

Above: Angle irons frame a burnished-steel door and house lights that cast their glow on the low ceiling of Joan Field's New York apartment. Columns and floor-to-ceiling mirrors conceal a coat closet.

Opposite: Burnished stainless steel, routed maple-ply doors, and a rustic, hand-hewn teak fruit bowl all reside happily together in this tiny kitchen. The cooktop is placed so guests can lend a helping hand across this long, lean counter of smooth, khaki-tinted concrete. The mirrored backsplash reflects good fêng shui by warning the chef when guests approach from behind and averting the danger of accidents

Previous page: An inviting sofa that stretches from wal to wall visually widens a long, narrow room in Karen Fisher's New York penthouse. It's deep enough to snooze on or to serve as a pad for overnight guests. A lean, mahogany-and-steel bookcase grounds an overscaled mirror framed in stainless steel.

If you say that size doesn't matter, the words barely cross your lips before you're stuck guiltily holding the lie. In our culture, size is status. One can read in the size of a home signs of prosperity, or at least good luck, because if you have a big space you must have the means to afford it. A large home broadcasts a promise of ease and domestic peace with ample privacy for each inhabitant. It provides a graceful escape from the public world. Size is contextual and can't be defined by square feet alone. What is generous in Manhattan seems stingy in Montana, and a student's living arrangements would never work twenty years down the road. If poorly designed, a vast number of square feet can feel more cramped than a spare, well-kept studio.

Of course size matters. But bigger is not always better, and good things do not always come in small packages. The physical constraints of a small shelter demand your attention, and that is exactly what imbues a space with soul.

Careful design is even more important to the success of a small place than to a large one. It has to be thoughtfully structured around the life that will fill it, and its contents should be deployed with care. Frequent cleansing keeps the space alive. Your experience of the space expands. You coax storage out of unlikely places. You activate the vertical dimension, filling it completely with your preferences.

A small space can have the intense clarity of a well-built ship or the mystery and play of a puzzle. It is more concentrated and often more complicated than a large space. And like a classic Freudian dream in which a single gesture stands for three things at once, a small home must condense the needs of a large home into fewer square feet.

Even in the tightest environments, mindful design will create rooms for work, entertaining, and relaxation that suit the inhabitant's patterns of living. Subtle adjustments provide people with what they really need rather than superficial decoration that gives temporary pleasure rather than a deep and subtle change, proving that design is a healing art.

Badly handled storage areas are a liability in a home of any size. This too can be changed. In addition to the analysis and careful layout of storage, we work with color and light. Each little event of a person's life, even one as mundane as removing a brush from a utility closet, can be heightened by careful arrangement of shelves and a flash of brilliant color on the interior walls of the closet.

Hybrid rooms and dual-function rooms are today showing up everywhere,

Acquisition

WHEN YOU CREATE A SPACE, THAT SPACE BECOMES THE MOTHER OF WHAT GOES INTO IT; EVERYTHING THAT IS ADDED BECOMES PART OF THE FAMILY. SOMETIMES YOU MAY WANT TO BUY SOMETHING THAT'S TOTALLY UNHARMONIOUS OR PERHAPS JUST AMUSING. THIS IMPULSE IS A GOOD ONE—IF YOUR ENVIRONMENT IS *TOO* HARMONIOUS IT MIGHT BECOME BORING. BUT ANY NEW ADDITION SHOULD HAVE A FAMILY FEEL, AS IF IT WERE MEANT TO BE THERE, OR AT LEAST MARRIED TO ONE OF THE THINGS THERE. HERE ARE SOME GUIDELINES TO HELP YOU MAKE DECISIONS THAT YOU'LL BE HAPPY WITH LATER ON:

- Do you need this object? Will you use it? Can you walk away from it?
- Will everyone in the house enjoy it? Will it pose a danger to children or pets?
- Have you measured the space it will have to fit into? Will it fit through the door, up the stairs, or into the elevator?
- Is it comfortable? (It should be.)
- If it is designed to do more than one thing, does it do all of them well?
- Does it squeak, hum, rattle, whoosh, or beep? If so, do you want it to?
- If it is secondhand, should you have it repaired or cleaned before it comes into your home?
- Does it feel nice to your sense of touch? Is it warm or cold?
- Some fabrics and woods have an odor. If this object has an odor, is it pleasant to you?
- When this piece has lived out its life in your home, will it be harmful to the environment?
- Are the methods of production in agreement with your values? Is it cruelty-free? Is it produced by underpaid labor? Is it made of recycled material? Is it produced by a corporation whose policies or politics are intolerable?
- Objects with lasting value are worth waiting for. If you cannot afford the thing you really want, ask yourself if you can wait for it. Novelty fades, but design integrity doesn't.
- Is it easily maintained? Washable? Expandable? Repairable? Are parts replaceable, and if so, are they easy to find? Will it hold up for as long as you want it to?

> Don't make something unless it is necessary, but if it is necessary, why not make it beautiful?
> —*Ann Lee*

but they have long existed in small spaces where constant transformation of function is a necessity, not a style. By exercising in the common room, dining in the kitchen, opening the doors of a thick partition to reveal a compact home office during the week, we use each room to the fullest extent and the space remains vigorously alive. And our desire to spend time in expansive areas like parks and museums keeps us strongly connected to the outside world.

It is important that your life in a small space be cleansed or you risk thwarting the flow of air, light, and energy. Careful editing and generous, useful storage areas in every room is key. Renew spatial and emotional audits regularly, as time or new acquisitions or changing styles can turn something that was once a pleasure into a burden. Keep things current.

I often hear stories of people moving to a larger space only to watch helplessly as it fills up again, as if destiny determined that no horizontal surface, corner, or drawer should remain empty for long. The proportion of goods to space has more to do with habits of buying and cleansing than with the size of any given space.

For many of us, the biggest problem is letting go of things. We have trouble separating the *sentimental* value of a thing from its *present* value. Consequently we find our homes crowded with broken things, ugly things, even things that cause painful memories—the last remaining butter plate from a set, a lone sock, a badly worn chair purchased on your first trip to Spain. Do you truly want or need these things around you? At the same time, you shouldn't feel that you have to get rid of something that truly enriches your life.

There are as many ways to eliminate clutter as there are reasons for it to accumulate, from draconian rules about how many jackets will be permitted in your closet to expensive storage systems. There is no one-size-fits-all approach —the specifics of clutter control are something you have to work out for yourself. I often suggest passing something—or two things—on each time you acquire something new.

Still, new objects will press at your door. Gifts arrive. A coffee table in a catalog promises solace. Food will almost definitely taste better on a new set of dishes. A particular bumpy yellow vase will improve your life in ways that only time can reveal. New books enter like ants filing out of cracks invisible to the naked eye. I can't imagine inviting people for dinner and not being able to shop

Opposite: In the Manhattan apartment of Joseph Calabrese, the kitchen peninsula has storage on both sides. To ease entry in a tight space, the corner of the counter folds into a handkerchief point. A tambour door creates an appliance garage on the right.

(continued on page 91)

84

The strong architecture of this room is reinforced and anchored by running the line of two existing ceiling beams down the wall to bracket the galvanized steel chimney breast.

Cle

EMPTIN

For sent
no longe
the love
into a siz
the poss
twenty y
also be
or the fe
lines to k

ACTUAL
est marg
trash in
kitchen,
rooms.
Consider
ing item
donate, s

CASTOFF
ing an ar
out it. A
storage
Giving it

MEMORA
often dis
timental
teacup o
one such
mer love

> If time and space are one, it follows that those of us who possess more space must necessarily possess more time. This apparently absurd statement makes sense if we interpret space not just as physical or physiological substance but rather as the extent of willed action.
>
> —*Robert Grudin*

(continued from page 84)

for one or two things for the table because that's part of the whole experience of entertaining, and it is important to let yourself do that.

Today, shopping and entertainment have fused into one. It is a modern outlet for the hunting and gathering instinct that provides great rushes of adrenaline accompanied by feelings of victory. In our culture, the combination of general prosperity and the cultural imperative to buy for fun keeps more things coming in. If you've got too little, you feel deprived, but if you've got too much, your possessions smother you. If you are able to maintain a balance between the excitement of possibility and the burden of excess, you will probably find yourself in a saner, happier place.

Even if you declare a self-imposed moratorium on acquisitions, you can walk in and out of shops without buying, as a type of reading. Each shop, whether a high-end boutique or a mass-market discounter, is a shopkeeper's interpretation of our requirements, and the merchant probably arrived at that interpretation through experience. I go into shops with a wide-open mind and do dry sponging—that is, just soak up the details. These visits are an assault on the sensibilities at times, but they help to wake up static thinking.

It is an incredible luxury to have at least one empty space in the house, be it a drawer or a tabletop, a wall or a closet. Especially when space is limited, a single area of emptiness allows you to breathe. When designing a space, I often add extra storage space or leave several walls blank so that the space readily accommodates new thinking and expansion. That way, if you fall in love with a piece of art in Madrid or Senegal you can bring it home.

Opposite: An Art Deco chandelier, cast-concrete key drop, and imposing artwork take command of the foyer and make a strong statement about the lifestyle of the occupant. According to fêng shui, it is inauspicious to see a bathroom as you first enter a living space. The door to the only bathroom in this 500-square-foot apartment was rebuilt without ornamental molding, creating the necessary illusion of invisibility. A cast-concrete key drop offers the satisfaction of knowing that keys will always be easily found.

Color Play

COLOR CHOICE IS VERY PERSONAL AND THE WAY COLOR PLAYS WITHIN A SPACE IS PURELY A MATTER OF CONJECTURE UNTIL COLOR LEAVES THE REALM OF ABSTRACTION AND GOES ONTO A WALL OR A SOFA. COLOR HAS A LIFE OF ITS OWN, CHANGING CONSTANTLY IN THE REFLECTED LIGHT OF AN ENVIRONMENT, VIBRATING AGAINST OTHER COLORS IN A ROOM. EVEN WHITE CAN PULL A CHAMELEON SWITCH FROM PARCHMENT TO SNOW TO GOLD, OR IT CAN TAKE ON A ROSY BLUSH, SUCKING UP LIGHT AND COLOR LIKE A BLANK CANVAS. COLOR AFFECTS SPACE AND MOOD DEEPLY, SO JUST AS YOU WOULD BE PREPARED WHEN CHOOSING A ROOMMATE, BE PREPARED WHEN YOU CHOOSE THE MAIN COLOR, AND SELECT ONE THAT PLEASES YOU WITH ITS EVER-CHANGING MOODS AND PERSONALITY AND PILLOWS.

Every color has a warm or cool vibration. Hot colors such as drenched purple, fuchsia, reds, oranges, and burnished browns bring the element of fire to a space. Icy blues, summery greens, and soft pastels tend to cool things down. Naturals, linens, taupes, and limestone are supportive and grounding. Grays and silvers calm the mind, but they need a counterpoint color so as not to become depressing. Black brings the water element into a room. In fêng shui, a room is considered more universally appealing if a delegate from every color group is represented, even if only in the most minor accent. For instance, in a room layered with textured naturals, cranberry pillows or splashes of indigo can happily coexist with amber and chocolate accents and a green plant. A good way to bring in color is through art.

The choice of paint finishes are many—including matte, satin, and glossy, as well as textured paints—and these and the variations of the surface to be painted will alter the reflective quality of a color. Artisan plaster and every color and grain of wood will bring out unique qualities in a pigment. (I like to stain woods so that they mop up the stain but still celebrate the quality of wood rather than lose the material by painting them. To do this, the wood grain must have a reasonable quality.)

To get a good look at a wall finish or a floor finish, purchase a small can of paint and try the color on a corner to pick up light and shadow. Then go back to look at it over the course of the day and in artificial light, so you can explore as many permutations as possible. I usually go one step further for my clients and do more than one sample, so there are a couple of options. Be patient, as you will live with these walls for a long time.

When you simply cannot find the color you like for floor or walls, buy two small tins of related colors and mix them half and half or one third/two thirds in easily reproducible ratios. This will enable you to mix a color that is uniquely your own.

To envision all the colors in a room as belonging to a whole, bring samples of fabric, trim, woods, and metals that you are thinking of incorporating, and try them with the walls and floor. Colors and materials have a strong life of their own and will guide you to throw out and replace the ones that obviously do not fit in with the grouping. An off color or texture in a room is as unwelcome as a brash guest at a quiet dinner party.

The most important thing to remember is not to be afraid. Strong colors can look ghastly in small patches, so if you like the color just go ahead and cover the walls and ceiling. I remember the groans from visitors when I was covering a showhouse room in copper fresco and only a tiny bit was complete. It ended up a sensual, welcoming retreat.

REFLECTION

BRIEF FLASH. BEAM BOUNCED FROM THE MIRRORED SPIRE OF
STEEL. SILVER CLICK OF A LIPSTICK CASE. THE GHOST OF THE
LOVER'S EYE. A TINY FIRE IN A BRASS FINIAL. TEASING DEPTH
REVEAL. SMOOTH SLICK OF WALL WHERE BALLERINAS TORQUE
ROUND DISTORTIONS IN COPPER BOWLS. THE BASS-BEAT
LAKE. THE FACE IN PARTS: AN EYE, A LIP. A SECRET DOOR TO

THE EMPIRE STATE BUILDING. KINETIC SWIRLS IN STAINLESS
ROOM IN A BLACK LACQUER TRAY. SILKY REFLECTION OF A
N A POLISHED FLOOR. A SLICE OF TREE IN A MIRRORED
N FLIGHT. STARS STARING BACK FROM A STILL NIGHT POOL.
THRILL OF A MIRRORED BALL. ELUSIVE SELF IN THE SKIN OF A
THE OTHER WORLD.

AT HOME
WITH
NATURE

The elevator doors open, and you step into the peace and simplicity of a cabin in Colorado. The space has the absorptive quiet of sand, a virtual desert of silence that gently presses against you, soothing your senses.

Like the pupil of an eye opening in the dark to perceive shapes that were invisible a few moments earlier, this space causes your sense of hearing to open to the low level of sound. The hush of wind pushing around the corners of the building outside forms a backdrop. Your own footsteps plant you in time and place. A cab honking in the street far below balances this dream state with the present like a voice heard from the depth of a good nap. What is more antithetical to the urban experience than silence? And yet silence is at its most precious when encountered as a pause in the midst of noise.

> The most sweet and tender, the most innocent
> and encouraging society may be found in
> any natural object.
> —Henry David Thoreau

Many of our purest memories of happiness, wonder, and fear are set in natural environments. To design spaces that are effective on this basic level is a challenge that is both humbling and thrilling. We can learn to live in harmony within ourselves and our environment—whether in a city or in nature—by plucking the best of both worlds and combining them in a harmonious whole that is our special, sacred living place.

Robert Redford's Manhattan penthouse is designed to be a refuge that will support a quiet interior life and accommodate a more public life in the midst of a great city. "I do like urban," Redford says of New York City. "It celebrates the best of communal energy and social-cultural interaction. I started my career here, raised a family here. I wanted to come here from California in the fifties. My love of nature and the West is an underpinning, but it is not exclusive." Drawn to the cosmopolitan experience, but rooted to the earth, Redford admits he is most comfortable in the vast sweeping terrain and mountains that surround Utah. Since neither vast stretches of land nor the peace of nature is easy to come by in Manhattan, our goal was to create a space that evoked some of this man's experience in the oudoors.

We obviously would not attempt to duplicate his beloved landscape in the living room; there's something depressing about literal re-creations of natural scenes, although they are probably inspired by a true longing for nature. You'll sometimes find them in restaurants or hotel lobbies—perhaps a waterfall with real plants and real water running down stone slopes into a pool. Despite the enormous attention that has gone into the arrangement of the foliage and other details, all you notice is how unnatural it looks. A metal grate can be seen through the stones. Dust collects on the leaves of a plant. Even the most convincing indoor installation of nature carries the potential of breaking down or going out of style. Underneath it all is the knowledge that the scene cannot replicate the changes inherent in nature.

The more lifelike the display, the more disappointing it will be as the seams reveal themselves and the whole thing disintegrates into a collection of flaws. It is not merely fake but strikingly dead, like a butterfly on a pin. What is so intriguing about the butterfly, in life, is its fluttering, looping flight.

Opposite: This carved stone basin transforms the morning's wash into a celebration.

Previous page: As the main access to this penthouse apartment, this elevator doorway has been enlarged with a bronze frame, which angles from the wall toward the door to make its narrow scale more coherent with the room. This, in fêng shui, is seen as expanding opportunity.

> Nature is a teacher that never deceives.
> —*Albert Pinkham Ryder*

Above: The wind whispers through grasses gilded by the setting sun.

Opposite: Ancient bricks form a fireplace topped by a beam from an eighteenth-century warehouse. A Tibetan wheel connotes continuity.

Previous page: French doors open onto terraces with well-kept gardens. The walls, ceiling, and massive columns of linen-colored plaster harmonize with the tones of the upholstery and the sheer, iridescent gold of linen drapes. All the colors of Central Park are echoed in Redford's New York space: moss, chartreuse, lichen, stone, and grass.

Nature isn't static. The light changes. The wind blows. Trees die, but then a patch of nameless blue flowers appears at the corner of the lot. Nature always regenerates itself and surprises us—the parts are always moving, and we flow with them. The fleeting quality is exactly what is so affecting about nature. We feel incredibly lucky to catch the passing show.

Human interpretations of nature should celebrate both the natural and the human. Instead of trying to re-create a landscape in the projects I design, I seek to capture the palette of a particular landscape, the fleeting shadows, the controlled randomness in the sound of rain, the rhythms of flames. With design, there are ways to capture the spirit of nature's transitions, which is why I love shutters and venetian blinds—they produce lovely shadows throughout the day, displaying the passage of time on your walls. A fountain need not be fashioned to look like a waterfall, but the sound of its splashing water will help to combat the stress of monotony.

Before Robert Redford bought this penthouse, it had been occupied by one individual for more than seventy years. It was a rabbit warren of small fusty rooms with multipaneled windows. Despite enormous terraces, there was no garden to create a connection with the sky and the air, and the views toward downtown and Central Park were obscured.

The first thing we did was to create a flow of rooms and courtyard spaces where he can discuss business, work through scripts, or spend time with friends. We added more intimate retreats with nooks for reading and thinking. The space now unfolds graciously with surprises tucked in here and there: a small room upstairs became a painting studio; the doors of the large bedroom open onto a small closed terrace on the roof that can double as an outdoor

Above: A ceremonial cast-concrete vessel and recessed outdoor step lights are unpredictable companions in a tiny powder room.

Opposite: Jerome Abel Seguin's table from Bali sits on a Tibetan rug, illuminated by a resin-and-steel lamp. Quarter-sawn oak floors are stained a shade between teak and walnut. Woven leather chair seats and backs are reminiscent of the American West. Outside, the terrace walls are painted a warm terra-cotta to deflect an otherwise cold northern exposure.

study. The wood-tiled roof amplifies the sound of rain; sitting under it you feel as if you have ducked into a lean-to on a difficult hiking trail. Just beyond the windows, the plants form a natural screen. Below, the canopy of trees in Central Park sways and changes color with the seasons.

It's not an appearance of nature that we're after, but the effect. The inconsistencies and honesty of raw materials like rough linen, patterned stone, and sandy plaster help to re-create the variations we find in nature. By contrast, a few highly designed fixtures and elements accentuate the rough easiness of these materials. An expanse of warm-colored raw linen neutralizes the sharp visual fragmentation of the city. The rough modulations in wood and stone remedy the slickness of plastic and the perfection of glass, the cool precision of steel.

While I embrace technology and the convenience and availability of mechanically produced things, too much of it has the disconcerting effect of making everything homogeneous and regular and smooth. We can tolerate only so much smoothness. We crave the irregularity of hand-carved wood or rough-hewn stone. In this penthouse, massive carved wooden furniture grounds and contains you. Fossils are embedded in the stone lining the steam shower. Against this forgiving backdrop it is fun for human beings to have something as perfect as an Arnie Jacobsen–designed faucet magically emerging from the mirror. This abundance of textures balanced with the refined faucet, the glass wall, and a voluptuous stone sink are a celebration of our role as both creator and humble observer.

I can imagine the mental effect of an environment as a series of snags and smoothnesses that we may not even be conscious of. Our response to nature isn't linguistic; it happens on a guttural level. It can be understood at once, yet because of the variation that belongs to the natural world, it continues to reveal itself in layers. If the materials of the space you create communicate with the body on many different levels, you've got something powerful.

NATURAL SENSU

ALITY

From the kitchen, a narrow staircase leads to the owner's private, sparsely furnished painting studio. An antique Javanese offering box provides an auspicious place in which to store remote controls of an audiovisual system. A deep arch troweled with warm, creamy plaster. Luxurious woven-silk drapes play with shadow and light. A chair lashed with rope, a mahogany table, and a thoughtful pumpkin squash.

Earth, Fire, Water, Air

WE ALL HAVE THESE ELEMENTS WITHIN US TO DIFFERING DEGREES. THESE IMBALANCES CAN OFTEN DICTATE WHAT WE NEED IN OUR ENVIRONMENT TO FEEL GROUNDED OR BALANCED. SOME PEOPLE NEED TO BE COOLED BY MATERIALS; OTHERS NEED TO BE WARMED UP. I OFTEN USE ONE MATERIAL MORE THAN ANOTHER TO BALANCE THE CHARACTER OF MY CLIENT. YOUR CHINESE HOROSCOPE AND YOUR AYURVEDIC BODY TYPE CAN PROVIDE SOME CLUES TO WHICH ELEMENTS YOU HAVE AN AFFINITY FOR.

EARTH The earth is our ground. Nothing in our minds doubts its solid, steadfast qualities. Earth soothes and centers us. Earth is represented in fired earthen tiles, the support of concrete, the quietness of stone, and the warm comfort of brick. The timeless satin of an artisan's plaster gives walls depth and resonance. Earth can be implied in the solid cant of an Egyptian column or the massive depth of an archway plastered in the colors of the soil—dun, sand, travertine, ocher, amber. If earth is not in a room, the room tends to float and appear like a stage set. We pass through it without feeling that we belong there. Earth locates us in our spaces and provides emotional weight in high-rise dwellings and reminds us where we come from. Earth is static and embracing; we deliver ourselves to its calm strength. A strong earth element in a project is good for people who move around a lot and work constantly with their brains. Earth reinforces the spirit of place.

FIRE Fire brings warm energy and life to a room. A flickering fire in an unlit room promises warmth and energy as we gather at the hearth like our forebears. Fire mutates and changes, fire is creative—the spark of energy. The Irish country people have a lovely expression: "There is no fireplace like your own fireplace." In Total Design, as in fêng shui, fire is light and light is fire. Light draws us into a new world that is neither night nor day. The white flash of halogen, the peaceful glow of a Noguchi paper lamp, the sparkle of chandeliers, the seduction of candlelight—each is a different type of fire.

Ring your room with light, like ancient people in their camps, so there are no dark corners where something alien could lurk. Bring energy into every corner with a simple lamp to cast light on your ceiling. Rim your property with light to give you a sense of safe territory.

The steady heat of an electric stove in a kitchen may bring the same service as a fire—it warms our stew—but the flicker of gas flames touches a more primeval part of our being. Microwaves simply respond to our frantic lifestyle; there is no visual pleasure.

Fire need not be literally present; poppy red, cinnabar, scarlet, burnt orange, and saffron will introduce the flash of fire into a room. The color of flame quickly ratchets up our energy on a dull morning. A room without fire lacks energy. I will paint the inside of a broom closet fire-engine red to provide a quick fire fix and to bring energy to the person who does the cleaning. Red is a good color for dining and dancing. If flame is missing from a room, the energy goes down.

WATER Water is liquid, transparent, and spirit-cleansing. Clear water in fêng shui implies prosperity and clarity. We came out of water and water is the main element in our bodies. The infinity of a reflecting pool and the splash of a small fountain will awake an answering tide in our bodies.

Designers will talk of a room needing "some wet." A mirror or a shiny surface can bring the element of water to a room through the reflection of movement and light. Black and dark green represent water in fêng shui. I place a fountain in every possible project. The sound of water is universally liked, so I tend to put water near the entrance of a home, as in the old houses in Kyoto, so that the sound ritually cleanses the soul as one enters or leaves. I watch people in airports perching around fountains and reading near reflecting

pools. Their body language softens near the sound of water. Even a beautiful hollowed-out stone on a table with a puddle of clear water in it will provide the sensation of water.

Fluid is the opposite of rigid. Rigidity is dangerous in this changing world. Flexibility and fluidity are qualities that allow people to move with the changes.

AIR Air is invisible yet vital. It can carry fragrant or noxious smells and is striated with invisible transmissions of sound, electronic vibrations, birdsong, and cricket and frog choruses. It can be busy, like an overdesigned carpet, or still and close like a cave. Air can become electric and unsettling before a storm or soft as silk on a spring morning.

Air should move and circulate freely with no stagnation. I use ceiling fans, cross ventilation, and, of course, air conditioning to bring the sensation of freshness to my projects. Like all the elements, air can be an ally or an enemy. Placing the bed near a window will allow a morning breeze to come in with the sun as a gentle wake-up call. Air will carry a waft of orange blossom or a palate-teasing hint of garlic. A ceiling fan quietly whirring will cool hot summer days. An attic fan will whisk out stale air on a suffocating summer day. A high ceiling or stairwell calls attention to volumes of air. We share the air with the rest of the flora and fauna of the earth. When you actively engage the air as a design element, you remember to breathe.

Easy Maintenance

A SPACE SHOULD BE ABLE TO WITHSTAND HARD USE. MATERIALS THAT ARE DURABLE AND EASY TO MAINTAIN FREE US FROM HAVING TO WASTE ENERGY WORRYING ABOUT HOW WE STEP ON THE FLOOR, HOW WE SET A CUP DOWN ON A COUNTER, HOW WE TURN A CORNER. I WANT PEOPLE TO ENJOY THEIR LIVES, NOT BECOME SLAVES TO THEIR ENVIRONMENT.

One of the easiest wall materials to maintain is artisan's plaster because it is extremely tough and durable. It has depth, mystery, and a rich satiny warmth. If you give it a ding it only looks better, like the wall of an old castle in Tuscany or Rome. In flooring, sealed stone and sealed concrete are tough, durable and solid. Aged steel continues to acquire patina. Wooden floors are warm and welcome use. Fabric can be washed, and when you get tired of it, you can replace it. For work surfaces in the kitchen, end-grain butcher block can be beaten-on and will retain its beauty while also having antiseptic properties.

The rougher rustic feel of these materials should be framed by a few articles that are more refined. It's the same principle that makes worn and torn denim jeans look so right with an absolutely clean and fresh T-shirt or a beautifully tailored shirt. The combination of rough and polished makes both look carefully considered.

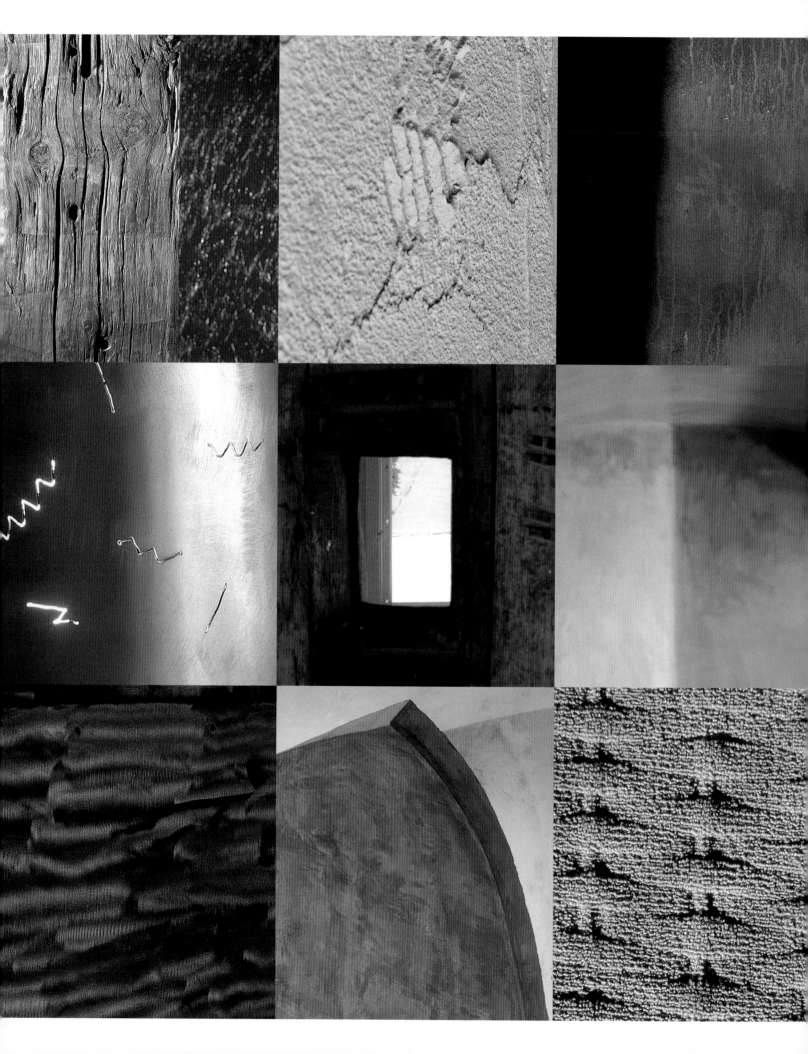

Materials

DECORATION COMES LAST IN TOTAL DESIGN. ROOMS ARE MADE BY THE INTEGRITY OF THEIR MATERIALS, AND THEY CAN STAND ALONE IN THE SAME WAY THAT AN EMPTY FARMHOUSE IN TUSCANY SEEMS PEOPLED. THE TACTILE QUALITIES OF MATERIALS AND THEIR INTRINSIC VALUE AND WEIGHT LEND VALIDITY AND LIFE TO A SPACE.

In the rooms I design, the inherent quality of materials is celebrated and layered to imbue surfaces with depth and resonance. The samples I keep in my library give me inspiration all by themselves: satiny plasters, flamed stones, slate, chunks of amber, teak, and dense concrete, a layer of golden scrim trapped between two layers of glass, a sensuous curve of cast bronze, a paint pot full of rich indigo.

Sometimes even this vast repertoire of textures doesn't offer the feel I crave. I will interfere with the surfaces of materials, applying a burnished patina to steel that makes it the color of an autumn leaf or grinding stainless steel so that it has all the joyous faceted qualities of a disco ball. I sandblast wood lightly or heavily to create surface and depth, or polish and wax it so it becomes mirror-dark. In my carpets and textiles I use flecks of reflective and metallic yarn to add depth, light, and mystery. I add mica chips to plaster so that walls look as though they have captured flickers of light. I backlight translucent onyx and marble to create seductive glowing lights. I laser-cut and water-cut bronze and steel and put flickering bulbs behind them to create kinetic screens.

Here are some suggestions for bringing the natural glory of materials into the foreground of your design:

- Where possible use simple natural materials: wood, stone, concrete, linen, cotton, wool. In my studio, we also use hard-wearing synthetics and acrylics. However, I work with an environmental consultant and deal with vendors who are aware of the potential environmental hazards these materials pose and who comply with environmental safety standards; if you are not sure how a synthetic is manufactured, better to pass it by.

- A long two-inch-thick stone ledge will lend glamour and weight to a radiator cover where a laminate would fail or simply look like a journeyman's solution. This ledge can be used as a buffet or to display a group of candles.

- Use wooden slats to cover a radiator. Their linear quality will help to organize a room. Wood venetian blinds will continue the horizontal rhythm.

- Place a plasma-cut steel screen in front of your television set when it is not in use. Leave it turned on with the sound off when you have guests. It will create a flickering show of changing lights.

- An etched art-glass panel a few inches wide can fit into a slot cut in Sheetrock, allowing light into a windowless bathroom. An opalescent glass screen will give privacy to a penthouse bathroom while bringing light from the exterior through to a dark corridor.

- A chunk of heavy cast concrete with a well in it forms a sculptural key drop in an entryway.

- Scratch-coat plaster creates a counterpoint to smooth limestone in a home spa.

- Polished artisanal plaster creates walls as powerful as art and lasts forever. This plaster can be applied over Sheetrock walls if a bonding agent is applied first and then a layer of scratch coat before the final satiny finish is troweled on.

- A stone hearth reinforces a fireplace.

- Rich blue chenille lends tactile qualities to a chair for reading. A thick velvet curtain drawn across a room creates an antechamber and a dense matte silence.

COLORS OF THE

DUN SPANISH SOIL. THE GIANT CRACKLE PATTERN OF
SUN OF AFRICA. PYRAMIDS OF TERRA-COTTA COOKING POTS
MALLEABLE CLAY AWAITING THE POTTER'S HAND. OXBLOOD
POLISHED BY GENERATIONS OF FEET. A GLEAMING ENGLISH
MOURNING DOVE. THE HOMEY CRINKLE OF BROWN PAPER
TOES. SEVERAL HUNDRED COLORS OF SNOW. THE ORANGE
DLES. A MOUND OF BROWN RICE. A DIRT ROAD IN ARIZONA
ABLE CLIFF. THE CREASED HIDE OF AN ELEPHANT SHOWERING
FLOOR. A HUMBLE PEANUT SHELL.

EARTH

PARCHED WATERING HOLES SUCKED DRY BY THE SEARING
A DARK SLICE OF EMERALD SOD FRESHLY TURNED BY A PLOW.
STAINED MUD-PACKED FLOORS IN NEW MEXICO. MAHOGANY
SADDLE ON A CHESTNUT MARE. THE SOFT GRAY OF A
BAGS. WARM MUD SQUISHING BETWEEN A CHILD'S BARE
SILENCE OF A FOREST FLOOR MATTED WITH OLD PINE NEE-
STRETCHING FAR BEYOND YOUR SIGHT. A COLD, UNASSAIL-
ITSELF WITH TRUNKFULS OF DUST. SAWDUST ON A SHOP

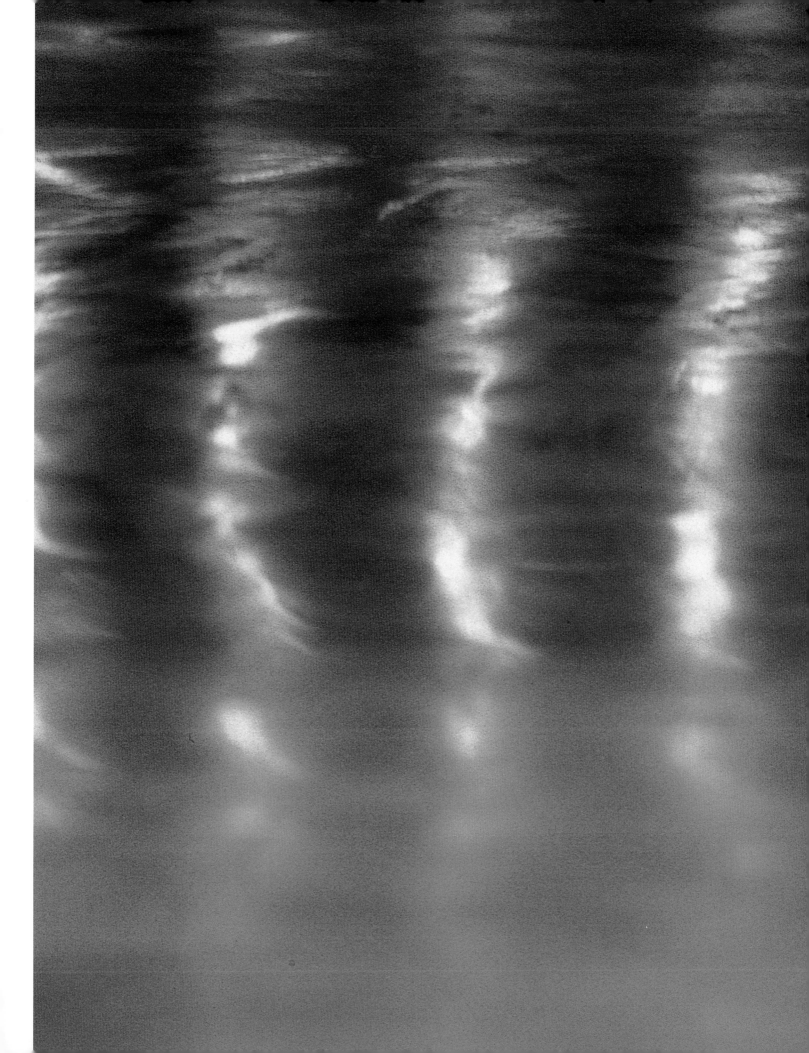

BRIDGING THE PRIVATE AND THE PROFESSIONAL

How does the person quietly reading in the privacy of a well-cushioned window seat become the executive striding toward her car and driver? And how then does she metamorphose into a gardener, kneeling in dirt, digging holes for hyacinth bulbs?

Most of our lives require us to shift from place to place. As we move between home and office, or between family spaces and an area designated for work in the home, our quality of speech shifts, our posture is altered, our energy level spikes with each change of environment. Each time we make such a shift, a small transformation takes place.

Life expands and contracts according to one's courage.
—Anaïs Nin

Above: Woven-steel wire cages create a modesty vest for an ever-changing technology.

Opposite: The reception area of Sylvia Rhone's Elektra Entertainment Group office provides a warm solidity and hospitality. A floating wall behind the desk is coated with an ocher plaster layered over bronze mesh. A custom rug swirls with musical icons. Steel, copper, bronze, and plush mohair reiterate the story of strength, energy, light, and music.

Previous page: Crimson-polished plaster reflects on the core walls within this seven-floor office suite, reinforcing a lively, joyous corporate image.

Both the private and the professional facets of the self, like the different rooms of a house, are extensions of a core. Whether we are in work mode or completely relaxed and "off the clock," our various modes and idiosyncrasies play off of one another, giving us depth and substance; their differences inform and contrast one another. The design of the physical spaces we occupy throughout the day should support these variations and help us to feel unified. When there is a vast discrepancy between our personal and professional arenas, a jagged, fragmented feeling is often the result.

We tend to create our own daily rituals to bridge the chasms between the different parts of our lives. It may be the simple act of making a pot of tea, taking a long soak in a hot bath, grabbing a cup of coffee, reading a newspaper on the subway, or spending a few minutes staring into space. Being conscious of your rituals imbues the commonplace with extra meaning. Environments built around these pleasures make each one into an opportunity for celebration. In my view it is the job of the designer to extrapolate the essence of a person and how he lives and reflect this essence in the design, whether it is for a private space or a professional one.

Unfortunately you can't design every space you enter, but you have a pretty good chance in your own home. If you have control over the design of your workplace, the same design principles should be applied there as well, providing more opportunities to explore the connectedness that makes daily ritual more meaningful.

The subtext here is that design—whether for a public or private space—should be an authentic expression of ourselves. Too often we show the world a different face when we are in our professional guise, a carefully neutral (or fictitious) persona intended to mask our idiosyncrasies and personal histories. Working surrounded by bland, generic furnishings, uniformly smooth, unfaceted textures, and nondescript industrial colors, our creativity is reined in, our spirits slightly deadened. Yet we feel most free to invent, to explore, most inspired in an environment that taps into our vast wellspring of nostalgia. For this reason, it is essential that the gap between *all* the spheres of our lives be bridged to as great a degree as possible.

The three spaces I designed for Sylvia Rhone, CEO and president of the music company Elektra, form a triptych that provided strong reinforcement of her character. She works very long hours and travels frequently. When she is

not on the road, she moves between her Manhattan office, her apartment, and a retreat on Martha's Vineyard. She loves her work, and she loves to entertain, relax, and spend time with her daughter. My goal was to help her retain a sense of harmony and integrity throughout each of her environments.

Rhone is a very decisive, creative person who knows herself and what she needs and wants from her living spaces. She knows how to edit out what doesn't work for her. These qualities made it much easier to achieve the kind of clarity she was looking for in the design of her homes and office. What is important to her is at the forefront: her family, her work, her heritage.

Rhone is quick to recognize that her life's hectic pace needs to be balanced by a sense of calm and retreat in all the environments she inhabits. To accomplish this, we linked the various spaces by introducing elements that are soothing and meditative. I learned that water is important to her and that she loves flowers and gardens and the soft, flickering light of candles. She needs relaxing spaces for conversation and room to entertain.

What happened in these three spaces is interesting because they all serve their purposes as home, office, and retreat, but more important they serve their inhabitants by blurring the barriers between those worlds.

Stepping inside her lofty apartment in Manhattan, Rhone is greeted by fantastic river views where walls used to be. In the foreground, trees are visible in one of her terrace gardens. Fountains gurgle in the background, and the reassuring symbols of her astrological sign and that of her daughter are embedded in the floor.

The space is clean and spare, yet it is earthy and filled with intense color too. Her African-American heritage is reflected in the art she collects and lives with, in stencils and hardware, and in the fabrics of cushions and carvings of furniture.

Rhone's working life is reflected in her vast music collection and the sound system, which is always available but hidden. Sound specialists have installed speakers everywhere. Music and television are important aspects of her working life that she also enjoys at home. In her muted, meditative bedroom there is a sitting area that makes it a place to be alone as well as to entertain or spend time with her daughter. Bathing is an important ritual to her, and in the bathroom there is a view of the Statue of Liberty from the tub and of the terrace plants from the glass-doored shower and ceremonial washbasin. Scented candles are everywhere.

In Total Design I try to imagine each of the rituals that carry us from one role to another as an opportunity to entertain a new part of ourselves. You may view this process as peeling off the outer protective layers or donning a different hat. Often the transformation requires some coaxing. I marvel when I contemplate the transformation that the business world undergoes each morning: a vulnerable soul rises from sleep, showers, dresses, eats breakfast, listens to the news, and then competently reenters the world, outfitted to face the day.

The path between worlds need not be so difficult to travel. We can carry

Above: In a window over New York harbor, the flicker of a sculpted candle echoes the distant torchlight of Lady Liberty.

Opposite: Evening sun brushes a large painting by Guattara.

Previous page: In Rhone's entrance hall, an ebonized anthropomorphic bench grounds a painting flashed with cobalt, graphite, and white. Water comes down in waves over a standing concrete fountain, and strong architectural shapes strike a harmony under a coat of polished mocha plaster.

130

In Sylvia Rhone's
Manhattan living room,
glowing lights flank a
window seat twenty-
seven stories above
New York, protecting
the fêng shui–like
sentinels at attention.

Above and opposite: Blown-glass lights rim the room in Rhone's Martha's Vineyard house with a soft glow, adding good fêng shui to this uncluttered family room. A deep-piled custom rug the color of warm sand invites you to curl up your toes. A large, canvas-sailed fan centered high in a kiva-like ceiling stirs quiet summer breezes and enlivens the chi in this auspicious octagonal room.

Overleaf: An overscaled steel-and-acrylic sconce glows at the end of a slender grass runway. The Mesa table is a slab of cast plaster and resin set on an oxidized steel base. What good design is all about: the enjoyment of life! A thirteen-foot sweep of concrete is set on an I-beam. Professional chef's tables form a trough of glass and steel and invite clients and the studio team to a working lunch. On a sea of old maple floors, translucent scrims stenciled with inspirational phrases and brick arches create a backdrop for Clodagh's showroom.

132

things back and forth if they are pleasing to us. I encourage clients to do away with their assumptions about what a space should be. Why should an office be a severe place? Our work can be tremendously enjoyable, and the functional needs of the environment do not demand that it be unpleasant.

Each morning, Rhone walks past an energizing brilliant red hallway on the way to her personal office. When she opens the door, the aroma of sandalwood greets her. Water is not possible in the office, but it is implied in the watery colors and textures of her office door. The colors inside are quiet and pale. Window boxes full of flowers grace every window. The place is a retreat within the larger office, which provides a place for reflection, to compose her mind and make her workday smooth and productive. A casual private conference room provides the intimacy for creative meetings that a large conference room doesn't allow. The corner placement of her desk, diagonally across from to the entrance door, is typical of fêng shui, setting her in a position where she can see everything and everyone that enters her office while protecting her from behind. There is a light in back of her but no art. Nothing competes with her for attention. The effect is strong. This is not your typical antiseptic office. It definitely belongs to this particular woman, and Sylvia Rhone is comfortable here.

In her Martha's Vineyard retreat, the feeling is casual. There are views of the sea, a real earth garden with a pond and a serpentine bench you can sit on to watch the sun set. There is an outdoor shower. The kitchen is larger here than in the city apartment because here Sylvia has more time to cook and entertain. Sea grass gathered from nearby dunes is embedded in the walls of the common room, giving the area a feeling of casual rusticity. The bedroom has the same Zen qualities, this time a soothing parchment, with a settee for reading.

A media room invites relaxation with its large, chunky sofas for watching television and listening to music, and a bar for convivial gatherings. African-inspired patterns and art are repeated in this home. Everywhere there are candles. There is comfort in contrast and familiarity.

As we move between worlds, the different spheres of our lives, we remain the same individuals, yet we seem different, even to ourselves. Interior balance is delicate, but harmonious environments true to who we are will help to keep you grounded and honest. Ask yourself: What are the coherent threads that run through my life, and how can I celebrate the different textures of my life by having them reflected in my environment? You shape your space and the space shapes you in a dance that becomes less about who's leading than about how the various parts flow together.

Home Office

YOU LIVE WHERE YOU WORK, AND YOU WORK WHERE YOU LIVE. THE BOUNDARIES BETWEEN OUR PRIVATE AND PROFESSIONAL PLACES HAVE BLURRED WITH THE EASE AND PACE OF MODERN COMMUNICATION. THERE IS NO SPEED LIMIT ON THE INFORMATION HIGHWAY. WE PHONE, FAX, AND E-MAIL OUR OFFICES, OUR HOMES, AND OUR LOVED ONES. THIS IS GOOD AND BAD.

Few of us leave work at the office anymore. We conduct business from cars, trains, and planes, from island hideaways and mountain retreats. We don't even leave the *office* at the office but carry around with us entire company files, Rolodex, calendar, dictionary, and message center in a three-pound computer. Yes, it's hard to get away from it all. But it's also very easy to bring it all home. State-of-the-art technology makes viable telecommuting, job-sharing, flex time, staggered schedules—the new order of the workday world that enables us to weave together home and career more seamlessly than we have since the Industrial Revolution put an end to the family farm.

This new and improved social fabric is a delicate blend. Home office is, after all, an oxymoron. Lest anyone lose sight of the essential distinction, I have set three inviolable ground rules for designing one:

- First and foremost, always have a divider separating your office from your home. It can be a door, a decorative screen, a curtain—anything as long as it creates a physical boundary and a visual barrier between your work space and your living space. Second, never have an office in the bedroom, even if you sleep alone. To work and sleep in the same space is counterproductive to both. Even in a one-room studio, you can fit a complete digital office in a closet or armoire and still close a door behind you at the end of the day. Out of sight, out of mind. Last, never share a desk. It is the ruin of a good relationship. I tell couples that even if a desk is 10 feet long, split it down the middle, get two of everything, and imagine there's an electric fence between you. It saves endless frustration and argument about never finding the thing you need in the place you keep it.
- The best part of having a home office is that no matter where you are on the corporate ladder, here you are CEO. In that sense, this is a fantasy room—the ultimate "room of one's own" to design as you please. How do you imagine yours? Is it a book-lined library with a cherrywood desk, leather sofas, and a fireplace? Is it an open loft with an industrial-size work surface and fabulous skylights? Is it a high-tech marvel with every new gadget in the sleekest design? For some, the idea of working where we live recalls that dread moment of childhood when we were summoned from play and banished to our room to study. Make your office the room of your dreams so that time spent there is a pleasure, not a punishment.
- Your location is a key factor in balancing your work habits with the family routine. Is anyone else at home when you work? Are sounds from the playroom or kitchen distracting, or does the background buzz help your focus? Do you need complete isolation or access? One working mother wanted a secluded space but did not want to be totally cut off from the household. We nestled her office under the crook of a stairwell, affording her privacy as well as a front door view to watch her children come and go.
- The dining room is often the least-used room in a house and is a good spot for an office, as long as it can be hidden in an armoire when dinner guests come. The dining table provides extra work space to spread out when you're alone.
- There are good reasons to have an office at home, even if you do not require it for your livelihood. An office by the kitchen or a well-trafficked passageway becomes a convenient information center for the family. Here is the perfect place to keep an answering machine, a message board, and the family social calendar. A home office can also be the family knowledge center—a hybrid library-study. Mine houses my book collection on healing and spirituality. I call it my literary medicine cabinet, and it is the first place I look for a remedy when a loved one is ill.
- Decide what furnishing and equipment you must have, then what amenities you want to add. Do you need a computer work station? A drafting table? A

separate entrance and work space for clients or colleagues? An intercom to monitor the door and communicate with the household? The first investment should be an ergonomically correct chair and efficient task light. Shop the design stores. Whatever you need, from telephone to tape dispenser, buy what you love in the best quality you can afford.

- Is your house adequately wired? A digital office with its floppy disks, CD-ROM, and compact multifunction peripherals greatly reduces the need for space but taxes a home electrical system. Make the necessary changes to handle your computer and telecommunication systems in addition to all your home appliances, and be sure you have easy access to concealed wiring for future upgrades. Avoid carpeting that may cause static electricity and use surge protectors with all your sensitive electronics.

- Keep your desk orderly, your tools sharp, and your files fresh. Label bins for in and out. Organize books by subject. Piles and stacks kill creativity. If your work is blocked, light a scented candle. Take a break. If possible, do reading or research on a garden hammock or poolside chaise; keep a chair and ottoman by a window view. I encourage my staff to leave the office; sometimes the ideal work space is a café table.

- Take steps to minimize outside distractions and make your space amenable. Good lighting is essential. Balance focused task lights with sconces or floor lamps—downlight compresses energy while uplight releases and enhances it. Create white noise. Have a fountain or listen to instrumental music. I put on Chopin and Miles Davis when I'm contemplative and reggae when I want to be revved up. You will better resist the siren call of the kitchen if you keep on hand a beautiful carafe with water or tea and a basket or bowl of fresh seasonal fruit. It makes a healthy snack for the midday doldrums and a lovely still-life in between.

137

UNPREDICTABLE

DETAILS

A mirror set into the peephole of an antique Dogon door reflects the morning. Backlit plasma-cut steel on a stair tread. African drumsticks lashed with wire give cabinet pulls an interesting twist. A weighty cast-bronze frame anchors a hammered bronze door.

Personalizing a Professional Space

AT WORK, YOU HAVE A RESPONSIBILITY TO RESPECT THE CORPORATE IMAGE, WHICH MAY REQUIRE SOME TEMPERING OF SELF-EXPRESSION. BUT IN ORDER FOR WORK TO WORK FOR YOU, IT MUST FEED THE SOUL AT LEAST A BIT, SO SOMETHING OF YOURSELF REMAINS AT THE END OF THE DAY. THE RIGHT BALANCE OF DESIGN ELEMENTS CAN HELP TO BALANCE THE SENSES AND DRAW US INTO OUR SILENT CENTER, WHICH IS THE SOURCE OF CREATIVITY AND SELF-RENEWAL. CLARIFY WHAT YOU REALLY NEED IN YOUR WORK SPACE TO BE PRODUCTIVE AND HAPPY. THEN CREATE IT USING THE IDEAS SUGGESTED HERE:

- Are you set up to get rid of correspondence and paperwork quickly and efficiently? Create an in-out box and a good filing system, which are essential to a clean, orderly work space. If organization isn't your strong suit, call in a friend or consultant. Use multi-colored folders. They help to identify files at a glance and add pizzazz to a mundane function.

- Empty your desk and cabinets inside and out of anything stale, broken, or outdated. These things are not only dust collectors and time wasters, but they also reflect poorly on your motivation and self-image.

- Letter boxes, tape dispensers, scissors, staplers, pen holders, paper clips—efficiency demands that you have these tools at an easy arm's reach. Utilitarian items can enhance your space instead of clutter it. Go to a museum shop or design store, and buy a desk set and accessories with clean lines and eye-catching hues. Today, even paper clips come in a riot of shapes and colors. The expense is minimal, considering the daily pleasure you get from using these objects.

- Invest in fine writing instruments. One beautifully crafted pen that feels just right in your hand is better than a fistful of Bics. A well-designed mechanical pencil eliminates the need for sharpeners altogether.

- Put your signature on interoffice mail by using stationery in your favorite color or distinctive materials. In my studio, a lime-green Post-it always announces a memo from my assistant. If I'm expecting papers from my partner, I know they've arrived as soon as I see the clear green envelope on my desk. Color coding makes identification quick and easy—and gladdens the eye.

- Fluorescent light is energy efficient only in electrical terms. Many people find it draining to work under and a strain on the eyes. Request management to provide you with a good task light. Even if you can't switch off the overhead fluorescent fixtures, the addition of incandescent or halogen lighting to the work space will boost human energy and output.

- Back pain and carpal tunnel syndrome are occupational hazards of the technological age. If you spend hours at a desk or computer and can order your own chair, get one that's ahead of its time in comfort and style. If you sit on standard office issue, at least make sure the seat and keyboard are the right heights for you. Consult an ergonomics expert.

- Have at least one chair for guests and, where possible, a table where staff and clients can work or play.

- Artwork on the walls makes a personal statement that may be inappropriate to the corporate image. Instead, use mirrors to create visual interest. If your desk faces a wall, mirroring the area between the desk and upper cabinets or shelves lets you see who is approaching from behind and preserves your power, according to fêng shui.

- If the only office windows are on your computer, use a screensaver picturing a skyline or landscape.

- Buy a meter to check air quality. Purifiers and humidifiers provide increased comfort and decreased risk of illness, especially where the windows do not open and you are breathing recycled air all day.

- An aromatic plant or a single fragrant bud in a vase provides a welcome biobreak from the unnatural pace and environs of an office. Orchids are ideal because the bloom lasts for months, and with proper care, these perennials flower again and again.

- No room for flora? A dab of essential oil on your pulse points can alter your mood. Lemon, ginger, sage, rosemary, and thyme energize; jasmine, geranium, rose, and sandalwood relax.

- Keep hydrated by drinking plenty of water or herbal tea. Carbonated and caffeinated beverages don't do the trick—in fact, they tend to be drying to the skin. Buy a flask and one beautiful drinking glass. A crystal highball glass provides a little sparkle and turns a plain drink of water into a delightful indulgence.

- Don't let on-the-job stress get the better of you. Do yoga, meditate, or get a weekly massage. Breathe deeply. Walk around. Smile. It signals the body to release mood-controlling hormones that can ease your state of mind before you are back at your desk.

- Pets relax people. If your workplace permits, bring in your dog. Cats may trigger allergies, so check out who has sensitivities before unleashing Fluffy on coworkers.

RED

THE VERMILION SPLASH OF POPPIES ON THE CORNFIELDS OF
AN ANDALUSIAN VILLAGE. THE VELVET CENTER OF AN OLD
ON GRAY, MISTY MORNINGS. A MATADOR'S CAPE. CARDINALS
TO DOWDY BEIGE. A FIERY MG ROARING DOWN A CURVING
JAPANESE MAPLE BURNING AGAINST A WALL OF SHADOWY
WAY. THE BARNS OF NEW ENGLAND. THE ROOFS OF PRAGUE
PILES OF BERRIES IN PROVENCE. THE HONESTY OF FINE BUR
MAHOGANY OF GINKGO BOWLS IN SEOUL. THE WINTER COM
HEDGEROW IN COUNTY KERRY IN SUMMER. THE EROTIC

FLANDERS. DARK PEPPERS GARLANDED BELOW THE EAVES IN
FASHIONED ROSE. THE GLEAM OF NEW YORK FIRE ENGINES
LIGHTING UP A BIRD FEEDER, TURNING EVERY OTHER BIRD
ROAD. A DEATH-DEFYING HIGH-HEELED SHOE. AN AUTUMNAL
YEWS. A PROCESSION OF TAILLIGHTS ON A FOUR-LANE HIGH-
AT SUNSET. THE RED STRIPES IN THE AMERICAN FLAG. LUSH
GUNDY. THE UNTAMED HAIR OF IRISH GYPSIES. THE GLOWING
FORT OF BORSCHT. CHERRY JELL-O. A BLEEDING FUCHSIA
FLASH OF A FRESHLY OPENED POMEGRANATE.

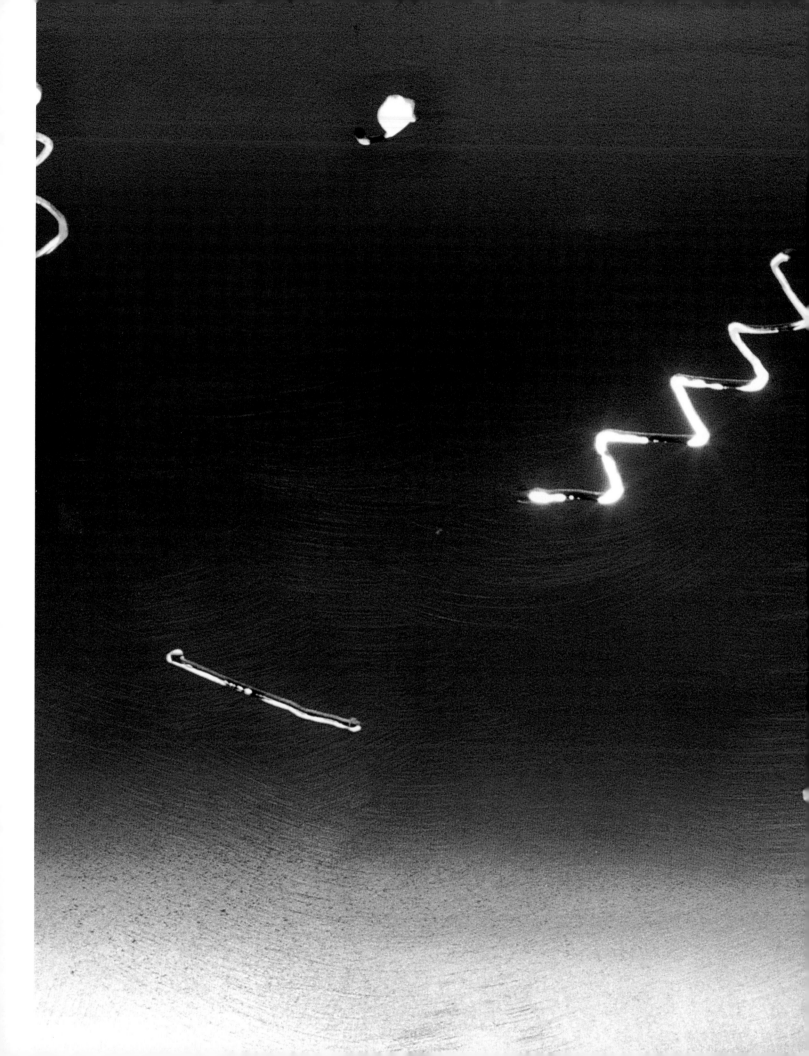

THE MUSIC OF SOLITUDE: CREATIVITY, PRIVACY, AND RETREAT

Each of us yearns for a space in which to create and for the privacy to discover our own voice. The level of privacy and solitude that each of us needs is personal. But in the safety of solitude, it is possible to tap into the creativity and vitality that is always within you.

The artist's demand for solitude is more pressing than most. The state of mind required to create works of art is famously fleeting, evaporating at the slightest environmental intrusion, a jarring car alarm, a ringing telephone, a circling fly.

And I shall have some peace there, for peace comes dropping slow.
— William Butler Yeats

Above: Woven into the texture of the garden, layers of grasses and white irises float like holograms around the bamboo-sheathed walls of a toolshed.

Opposite: Gauzy white sheers let in sea breezes in this bedroom retreat. A low chaise invites reading and contemplation, while a bronze candelabra with the patina of ancient Greece wafts fragrance and flickering light.

Previous page: Twenty-seven stories above Manhattan, this bedroom retreat melds the quiet and the bold. Chianti linens and a Wenge bed stand out from a softly brushed, patinated steel radiator cover that serves as a plinth for an African sculpture. An opalescent glass wall conceals the bathroom.

Though we may not all make art in the literal sense, we are all creative beings. It is intensely important to have time to oneself—ideally, a separate space for each individual where there is no possibility of even a passerby derailing one's thoughts. The textures of privacy are as various as the textures of social life. Some people need very little time alone to replenish themselves. Others crave social interaction only as a way to enrich their full interior life.

Cultural attitudes toward privacy and solitude are in constant flux, shifting from year to year and from culture to culture. It wasn't until the nineteenth century in England that our current concept of privacy regarding bodily functions and family life were widely adopted. Now, at the beginning of a new century, we are nothing if not an amalgam of borrowings from whichever culture and period suits us. This great freedom carries with it the responsibility for making choices about our position in relation to what is outside of ourselves.

Yet we are amazingly adaptable; even when there is no physical space in which to be alone, the solitude comes from within. In Japan, the walls in many homes are shoji screens, which provide visual privacy while allowing you to hear what is going on in the other parts of the house. Even on the subway in New York, you can see the shutters closing across people's faces as they disengage from the throngs around them.

Of the various activities that require privacy, those involving bodily functions get the most press, but that kind of privacy is the easiest to come by. The soul is much more demanding than the body. It requires a kind of privacy that is deeper and more complete. The private rituals we engage in when we are alone in a familiar environment let us maintain our spiritual lives and give us a chance to reestablish who we are and what is most important in our lives. In your own home, a few hours of privacy lets you ease back into yourself. No solitude is more replenishing. You are released, free to scratch, eat, snore, groom, cry, think, invent, and create. You can be silent or strange. You can test things out before setting them loose on the world, knowing the home will protect and support you.

Much of the negotiation that goes on in shared homes centers around issues of privacy. The interior of the home mirrors, on a miniature scale, larger cultural divisions between the public and the private. Shared rooms such as the common room, dining areas, and kitchen function like public courtyards. The bedroom, bathroom, and dedicated rooms become the inner sanctums within which even smaller, more discrete sanctums can be designed.

Living alone does not erase the need for these variations in how we occupy different areas in the home. If you have a space to yourself, the negotiation is internal, but the various modes and degrees of solitude are still there. A common room in a one-person home is still a theater in which you are both actor and audience. In contrast, a serene workroom with good light and a comfortable place to read helps you remain in your own thoughts.

In the homes of two extremely creative individuals, Herb Alpert and his wife, singer Lani Hall, our design mission was to bring into being retreats that would serve as backdrops to the work and leisure time of these musicians who also paint, sculpt, and write. The couple was searching for an environment without distraction for each space they occupied.

The issue of private and shared spaces was especially important because both husband and wife work at home. In their main house, for instance, we created separate music rooms. Sound isolation was important. An artist needs to be able to make noise that only he can hear and to make mistakes without an audience listening in. Likewise, the rest of the household needs isolation from the practice sessions. In another of the Alperts' homes we used the natural sound barrier of a closet full of clothing between the bedroom and the music room to allow one person to sleep while the other composed. In addition to these private areas for music, we designed a painting and sculpting studio and a special study for meditation and writing.

The shared spaces were just as important as the personal retreats. In the main house the common rooms were designed to be filled with friends and family. There were many huge, comfortable sofas and generous tables to gather around. In two of the other homes, we added fireplaces because in their main house the hearth had become an important meeting place where they would come together for conversation at the end of the day. In *The Unquiet Grave,* Cyril Connolly wrote that "marriage is a continuing conversation," an apt description of this marriage.

In both the public and the private rooms in the Alperts' homes we were looking to eliminate distractions. Minimalist environments are another way to edit out distraction and create freedom for self-expression. In the context of Total Design, minimalism is about luxury, not deprivation. Its aim is to surround you with the clarity and ease of a few well-chosen things. It lets the inherent beauty of materials shine in their full glory. Most important, a minimal environment does not compete with or constrict the creativity of the human beings within. This couple's homes are very stripped down. These spaces function well for working and entertaining in these cities. In New York, where the noise and pollution and stimulus from the environment are especially relentless, their home is a counterpoint, as still and quiet as a clay vase.

In especially stressful lives, no room is more luxurious than a bedroom stripped down to the bare essentials. There is a bed, of course, a chair for sitting, lamps for reading, a rug for warming the floor and absorbing sound. There

Above: A calm and nostalgic glimpse of the sunlit garden is one of the pleasures enjoyed when living in a transparent dwelling.

Opposite: On a teak table that is as happy inside as out, this little retreat set between gardens calls for migratory dining.

Previous page: A Tibetan rug is layered over wall-to-wall carpeting the color of camel hair. Monochromatic textures build up to create a sensual retreat. A seductive bed in a wood-paneled room, charcoal cast-glass lamps, the stacked glowing halos of a paper light shade, and the soft roll of the ocean. In fêng shui, a beam running lengthwise over a bed separates the occupants, but light cast both upward and downward, as well as flutes not visible in the picture, symbolically cures the oppressive effect.

153

should be a flower for fragrance and beauty, a window to drench the room in light and remind you of the world outside—and of your safe distance from it. No excess or decorative objects steal from your attention. In such a space, your thoughts and your surroundings merge, and you almost become delightfully transparent.

Even by the Pacific there is a need for a space of isolation from external stimuli. The Alperts' California guest cottage has been transformed into a Zen-like retreat. At 20 by 40 feet, it is the size of a swimming pool, and with one room, it is a truly minimal accommodation. There is a bed out in the open and a large round window that looks out to the garden; the sound of pounding waves is audible through a grove of pine trees. When the shades are closed in the daytime, a golden light comes through, and you feel as if you are living inside a lantern. This is where the couple goes to get away from it all.

Multiple spaces invite a designer to engage in themes of repetition infused with the variations that each location brings to a design. In each of these places, themes of sensuality, color, and comfort reemerge. The elements that remained consistent were how the spaces were to be used, a high level of comfort, and protection from the environment. Unlike the outside world, it is possible to control what you see, hear, feel, breathe, and swallow in a domestic space.

The goal of the music rooms in each home was to ensure solitude but also stimulation. We used a lot of vibrant color in the main music studio to rouse and almost agitate the musician. This is counterintuitive. We assume that artists need absence of stimulation and color, but the excitement and vivacity of the rooms resonates loudly and drowns out intrusive thoughts as well as sounds.

While each location, each home, comes with its own set of stimuli, and you want to celebrate those differences, a thread of continuity is still important for a sense of balance. We put the same comfortable mattress and plush towels in each one of the homes. The very same chairs for husband and wife are found in several different environments. Like spotting the face of a dear friend in a foreign city, it is reassuring to find familiar elements in the various places you live your life.

For each new space we asked the same questions, which you can ask yourself: What do you need? What do you want? What can you discard? What key element is necessary to make your life work? While the answers may not be exactly the same for each home or each room you inhabit, the process of gaining more clarity, of minimizing distraction, is crucial for the creative being you can and will be.

154

Above: Sunlight and chenille, sky and trees.

Opposite: A retreat can be for one or two or shared with a group of loved ones. A glowing, sentinel light column brings fêng shui energy to a dark corner of the room, while comfortable armchairs and a deep window seat encircling a massive low table invite long, intimate conversations in the ever-changing light reflected from the sea.

An organic wood
sculpture partially
screens the sitting
room from the dining
room. The seating
arrangement is
grouped conversation-
ally, adhering to West-
ern and fêng shui
standards alike.

Generosity

GENEROSITY IN DESIGN IS ABOUT HAVING ENOUGH—ENOUGH SENSORY STIMULATION, ENOUGH EMPTI-
NESS, ENOUGH STORAGE, ENOUGH CHAIRS, ENOUGH FLOWERS. THIS KIND OF PLENTY IS EASIEST TO
ACHIEVE WHEN YOU HAVE A LOT OF SQUARE FEET, BUT GOOD DESIGN CAN IMBUE EVEN THE TINIEST SPACE
WITH A FEELING OF BOUNTY. AND REMEMBER THAT ENOUGH MEANS EXACTLY THAT, NOT *MORE* THAN
ENOUGH. THOUGH IT MAY NOT SEEM OBVIOUS AT FIRST, SIMPLICITY IS USUALLY MORE GENEROUS THAN A
ROOMFUL OF SMALL, ORNATE SHAPES. IF A DESIGN IS TOO FINISHED-LOOKING, YOU MAY NOT FEEL THERE'S
ANY SPACE FOR YOU. TOO MANY OBJECTS IN A ROOM WILL MAKE YOU FEEL AS THOUGH YOU HAVE TO
SQUEEZE YOURSELF BETWEEN THEM. TWO SMALL TABLES IN A ROOM, FOR EXAMPLE, CAN CRAMP THE
SPACE WHEREAS A SINGLE LARGE TABLE WILL GIVE YOU ROOM TO SPREAD OUT. HERE ARE SOME IDEAS FOR
STRIKING A BALANCE BETWEEN ENOUGH AND TOO MUCH.

ONE OR TWENTY

- Numerousness and repetition play a big part in a home's generosity. But abundance suits some objects better than others. You want one table and twenty apples not three tables and two apples.
- If you are buying flowers and your budget is limited, buy a lot of daisies rather than a single rose. Three vases of tulips on a table give a feeling of splendid generosity. You rarely get the same splendid feeling from a lot of mixed flowers.

BIG SHAPES, CLEAN LINES

- Large-scale simple pieces in unpredictable locations will create impact and a feeling of generosity. By this I do not mean to make a feeling of sterility but one of clarity.
- Place one huge painting in a study, taking up an entire wall if necessary.
- A ceiling vault will create architectural form and visual excitement without taking away floor space.
- In a small bedroom, an oversize piece of furniture, such as a massive secretary, an armoire, or a four-poster bed almost the size of the room, is more generous than small-scale furniture that gives the room a doll's-house aspect.

ORNATENESS AND EDITING

- Limit the number of ornate objects in any given room. Part of their power is their intensity, but three or four will compete with each other, creating visual noise rather than visual interest.
- If you love opulence and ornateness, bring it in by layering sumptuous textiles and patterning your walls. Try a stencil on plaster, for example, rather than wallpaper. Ikats, Oriental rugs, Indian print brocades, and velvets bring sensuality and stimulation to a room. Don't hold back—one strong gesture needs another.
- Hang photos of your family and friends so close together that they form a collage.
- House collections in a confined area so that the collection becomes like a single art piece. Collectors who want to go on collecting should leave some space for additions.

STORAGE

- I cannot stress often enough the importance of sufficient storage space. Built-in storage areas offer a place to hide things that you do not want to display, like cleaning supplies, boxes of food, electronics, seasonal clothing, and sports equipment.
- Open shelving works better if there is a lot of it. It has a particularly honest quality. Just as the Puritans eschewed window shades as a way to keep their behavior seemly, open shelving lets you survey all that you have, for better or for worse. An entire wall of steel bookcases will look great; small bookcases dotted here and there look stingy.

PLAYFULNESS

- I never fully trust someone whose home does not contain at least one toy.
- Place a chalkboard in a guest room with a welcome message; choose a computer screensaver that amuses you; put a stack of *New Yorker* magazines by the guest bed.
- In a subtle space, humor can be subtle too. Every room can contain one object that upon close inspection is slightly out of step: a bright red chair, a small house in an otherwise decorous fish tank, a painting with a visual joke.

Windows

IT IS SAID THAT THE EYES ARE THE WINDOWS ON THE SOUL. IN THE TOTAL BODY OF A HOUSE, FUNCTION-
ING WINDOWS ALLOW LIGHT AND AIR TO FLOW IN AND STALE AIR TO FLOW OUT, BECOMING THE LUNGS OF
THE BUILDING AS WELL AS THE EYES.

Every window has its own integrity. I consider everything, from the window frames to the curtains or
blinds, to coax out a window's full potential. When I
begin a new project, I walk through the house observ-
ing the movement of the sun. I place seating where
people can warm and wake themselves with light and
air. I use veils and blinds to provide shade and privacy.

When I came to the States and first heard the
expression "window treatment," I was highly amused.
I envisioned a circle of physicians looking at the
offending window and discussing the pros and cons
of its cure. Now that I live here, I find that this vision
is not far from the truth! But overdressed windows
are like overdressed people who do not trust their
function and their intrinsic beauty. The simplest treatment of a window is often the best. Dressing it is the
final touch.

TYPES OF GLASS

- If you are installing new windows, consider different
  types of glass. Thermopane keeps out unpleasant
  noise and is energy-efficient as well. If you live in an
  area prone to earthquakes, check into shatterproof
  glass.
- Glass comes in a great variety of colors and textures. Its opacity can range from opaque to clear.
  Glass can be inlaid with wire or sparked through
  with bubbles. Frosted glass is translucent. Glass can
  be etched in graphic or organic patterns. Decorative
  glass can be set into a window that will not open.
- Check the color of any existing window glass to see
  if it will affect your interior colors. Many high-rise
  apartments have windows that are slightly grayed,

which has an effect on color, so you should check
paint and fabric colors within the space. Bring large
samples of color to your home.

FILTERS

- The sun can be our friend or our enemy. Special sun-
  filtering films filter out certain light waves, altering
  the quality of light that is admitted, as well as what
  can be seen outside. They can be purchased at a
  home improvement store.
- A good way to make sure that your upholstery and
  drapes resist fading and rotting is to apply UVL-
  filtering film to existing windows to cut out ultra-
  violet rays.
- If what lies outside of your window is unappealing,
  clerestory windows placed above eye level let the
  light in without the distraction of a view.
- Do not hang art in direct sunlight without applying
  either UVL-filtering film or another coating material
  called Solarveil to the window glass. These materials reduce damaging rays and decrease glare. They
  also veil the view from the window in a beautiful,
  mysterious way.
- A high window made of dichroic glass will cast rain-
  bows on your floor as the sun comes through.

WINDOW TREATMENTS

- Keep window dressings spare and clean. One kind
  of privacy or sun-blocking window treatment is usually enough. Occasionally there is a practical need
  for both drapes and shades, or both blinds and curtains, but visually, most windows look better with
  one or the other.

- If you need total darkness in order to sleep, use a blackout shade on a track that extends past the window so that no light leaks in.
- Some simple treatments that I've found to work well are wood-slat venetian blinds, which throw amazing striations of shadow on the floor; simple curtains made of fabulous materials and translucent pull-down shades in warm colors that create privacy while allowing light to come in.

TROUBLESOME WINDOWS

- Windows looking out on a neighbor who looks in at you can make you feel like a spectacle. Hanging sheer curtains or applying a filter to the glass will allow light in while masking the view in both directions.
- If a neighbor can see into a very private room, like a bedroom or bathroom, hang wood-slat venetian blinds that can be oriented to let you see outside without letting your neighbor see in.
- In a shower or bathroom, use frosted window glass above eye level, so that the user can enjoy sky and trees without being observed.
- When a window gives out onto a dark air shaft or neighboring building, use plantation shutters or wooden venetian blinds. Install a bar of light set into a trough at the top of the window, between the shutters and the glass, to cast light through the slats and enliven a dark room.

PICTURE WINDOWS

- A fixed, frameless sheet of glass in a window opening can be used to create a living artwork if it is placed where there is a garden or tree or something really special outside to look at.
- A plate window that frames a sweeping view of a landscape or cityscape is a classic pleasure. But don't always look for the obvious. Low windows give an intimate view of earth without sky. A low view of bamboo and river stone, or of a rock garden, is a wonderful surprise.

INTERIOR WINDOWS AND DOORS

- A piece of carved or etched art glass in a bathroom window will give total privacy and an indoor view.
- A long window cut into the upper portion of a wall will link two rooms together visually while allowing them to remain physically discrete.
- Amber glass set into slots in hallway walls will provide a warm glow in unlit areas.
- Full glass doors provide aural privacy while allowing the energy to flow through a building. They are inviting and function as a preface to whatever lies behind them—a sliver of what will happen within.

SKYLIGHTS

- Skylights let in light, and sometimes even air, without visual pollution. I install them wherever and whenever I can.
- Place architectural lamps outside, so they shine into a skylight, simulating moonlight.
- In Spain I learned to use skylights that were set behind a column or wall, so that they could not be seen, causing their light to flow down the walls as if from a mysterious source.

Guest Room

SUPPLY EVERYTHING THAT GUESTS MIGHT ASK FOR, SO THAT THEY DO NOT HAVE TO ASK. THE BIGGEST PROBLEM IN MOST GUEST ROOMS IS THAT THEY DOUBLE AS A STORAGE SPACE FOR DETRITUS AND JUNK. IF YOU HAVE TO USE YOUR GUEST CLOSET FOR YOUR OWN THINGS, CONCEAL CLOTHES NEATLY IN A HANGING BAG AND LEAVE ROOM FOR HANGERS FOR YOUR GUEST. IF YOU WANT TO ADORN THE GUEST ROOM, A GOOD MIRROR IS BETTER THAN A SO-SO PAINTING OR CHEAP PRINT. EVEN THOSE OF US WHO HAVE TO FIT GUESTS INTO A LIBRARY OR HOME OFFICE CAN MAKE THEM COMFORTABLE. A SCREEN OR A WELL-PLACED DRAPE WILL PROVIDE PRIVACY AND ALLOW A GUEST TO SLEEP A LITTLE LATER WITHOUT FEELING EXPOSED. START WITH THE FOLLOWING:

- A comfortable bed with a duvet and two pillows, one for reading and one for sleeping. I use soft down for the sleeping pillow and a firm oversize pillow for reading.
- A warm throw.
- Good adjustable bedside lights for reading.
- A bedside table for either side of the bed, or a ledge along the back of the bed.
- A closet or armoire with at least twelve decent matching hangers, plus six skirt hangers and a couple of shelves or drawers.

Once you've covered these basics, add more intimate touches to convey your caring:
- A tray with a flask of cold water and as many glasses as there are guests
- A scented candle. Lavender and lemon are unisex.
- A basket of amenities such as you would find in a boutique hotel: a comb, a brush, disposable razors, emery boards, Q-Tips, dental floss, toothbrushes, toothpaste, shoe polish, shampoo, body lotion, aspirin, Tiger Balm, tea tree oil, liquid soap, tampons, and condoms.

- A bath towel, a hand towel, and a facecloth for each guest.
- Robes or sarongs that can be tied on.
- A folding suitcase stand.
- Fresh flowers or a bud in a bud vase.
- One table with a small drawer holding pencils, paper, envelopes, postcards, and stamps.
- A local guidebook and map. A weekly guide to local events.
- A new magazine.
- A handful of paperbacks that you have finished. So often I have started a book at a friend's house and had to leave it there when I was half through.
- A small bowl of fruit and a couple of packages of nuts or a granola bar.
- A list of useful nearby services. I keep the list in my computer and update it regularly.
- A phone jack for e-mail.
- A duplex outlet at desk height so that the poor guest is never on her knees hunting for an outlet for her laptop.
- A compact radio–CD player with a few CDs.
- If there is room, a couple of armchairs, a side table, and a small TV set.

STONE

MUSIC OF WATER

TRANSPARENCY

LIMPID WATER BURBLING OVER RIVER STONES. A MARTIN
FRESHLY WASHED WINDOW. A DRIFT OF DIAPHANOUS CUR
FALLS IN WINTER. A VASE REFRACTING A BUNDLE OF TULIP
SEA. THE THOUGHTS OF A CHILD. AN IRIDESCENT SOAP BUB
LONDON PARK SEEN THROUGH A SCREEN OF FOG. A VELVET
THROUGH A CUT-CRYSTAL PLATE. THE TINKLE OF ICE CUBES
WINDOWS. THE SMOLDERING FLAME OF A SAINT'S CAPE IN
HAIR BEHIND A SHADE. A CELEBRATION OF CHAMPAGNE. THE
NEW LEAVES IN MAY. THE SHADOW OF A BREAST THROUGH
CHIFFON. A RUSTLE OF CELLOPHANE. THE MOTHERLINESS OF
GLASS-BOTTOMED BOAT. THE MAJESTY OF ORGANZA. THE

WITH A SLICK OF LEMON OIL. THE CRYSTALLINE PURITY OF A
TAINS. THE AMBER SEDUCTION OF PORT. FROZEN WATER-
STEMS. FRESH AIR. ORANGE CORAL WRINKLING IN AN AQUA
BLE. THE FIERCE GLINT OF DIAMONDS. HALOED LAMPS IN A
FRAGMENT OF BEACH GLASS. THE WARMTH OF WOOD
N SUMMER. INTIMATE NIGHT VIEWS THROUGH SUBURBAN
STAINED GLASS. A WOMAN IN SILHOUETTE COMBING HER
SMOKY VEIL OF A PORCH SCREEN. A GLOWING OVERLAP OF
SILK. THE GOSSAMER OF DRAGONFLY WINGS. A FLUTTER OF
SARAN WRAP. A MILKY SWIRL OF OPAL. FISH SIGHTINGS IN A
ETERNITY OF A CRYSTAL BALL.

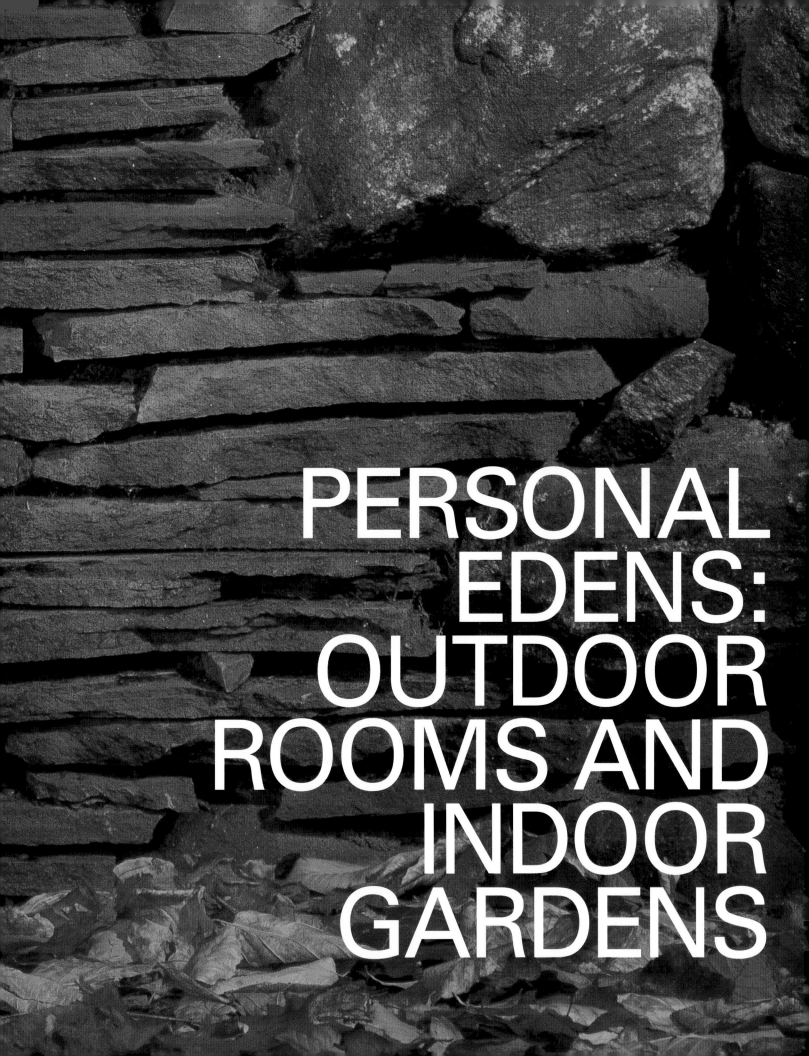

PERSONAL EDENS: OUTDOOR ROOMS AND INDOOR GARDENS

In the cultivated patch where nature and civilization meet, there is a tiny world made in the image of the gardener. In droughts, blights, and springtime resurrections, the gardener is reflected as she enacts, in miniature, the eternal struggle between wonder and control. The garden is never complete—it staunchly defies perfection and remains a work in progress. This is its most generous feature.

All things counter, spare, original, strange,
Whatever is fickle, freckled (who knows how?)
With swift, slow; sweet, sour; adazzle, dim;
He fathers forth whose beauty is past change.
—*Gerard Manley Hopkins*

Opposite: A small, unexpected Zen garden tucked under a sunlit stairwell slows the running of footsteps, offering a found moment of quietude.

Previous page: The use of commercial fabrics in residential spaces is sensible when pets, children, and spilled coffee are constant possibilities. Here, Avora fabric in midnight blue clothes an ample chair. An ancient Chinese water rug warms the floor, and a trough of emerald grass brings the outside in. A candelabra adding flickering light to the corner creates good fêng shui.

"Garden" in Total Design is a loose term. Tradition places the garden outdoors, but it is a small step to extend your domestic space outside or to bring something from nature indoors. A garden can be as modest as a small green statement on a central table, or as low-maintenance as a box of fine sand carefully raked around black stones. A tray of bright green grass growing on a windowsill is playful and simple. A night garden of moonflowers and conifers is the perfect place to sit after work; a low bench and a pool full of lilies and bright orange fish is soothing. Anything that calls and connects you to the rhythms of nature will do. For an especially disciplined Buddhist, a single blade of grass swaying by itself in the breeze might even work.

Total Design reimagines the garden as an outdoor room. Its contents do not differ radically from that of other gardens, but the focus of its design is to support and enrich you in your particular life. The garden should remind you of your own flexibility and resilience. A carefully landscaped plot of land can make a small house feel generous and a large house feel gloriously spacious. Your outdoor room will expand the space inside while giving you a feeling of connectedness with the world beyond the walls.

I apply the same criteria to the design of outdoor rooms that I do to interiors. Gardens are as various as the imaginations that compose them out of a spectacular palette of living and natural things, the elements, and human inventions; they may be as utilitarian as a vegetable garden or as abstract as the wind gardens of China.

When you nurture a garden, you dance with forces beyond your control. It is hard to remain self-contained when your hands are working in the earth; the universal connection becomes clear. The more stubborn the soil, the more pleasure you find in each petal. Obviously not everyone can or even wants to garden, but behind each person digging in the earth stands a crowd of grateful nongardeners: garden sitters and strollers, those who watch from afar, and others who are drawn like bees to fragrance and beauty. A life without some kind of garden is smaller for it. Those people who are too busy to imagine having time to spend in a garden are perhaps the ones who need it more than anyone. Gardens have a way of making room in an overcrowded mind. And if you have forgotten their purpose, visit one with a child.

There is much to learn and to borrow from the outdoor spaces of other cultures and eras. Romantic-style parks in nineteenth-century England were not for refuge but for dramatic display of wealth. Water and cypresses in Muslim parks provide oases of beauty in an earthly desert. Geometric French gardens, through serious tenacity, strong-arm flowers and trees into precise patterns. Chinese gardens are a celebration of the sublime beauty in a world where humanity is but one of a thousand things. The fruit trees in the sprawling gardens of the Taj Mahal were planted to give shade and food to the poor. Symbolic gardens of Japan can be read like literature. The American lawn is a peculiar kind of garden where uniformity reigns and each blade of grass is encouraged to be identical to its neighbor.

I recommend that some sort of garden be included in almost every project I take on. In the city, a garden provides an important contrast to the hard landscape of concrete, steel, and glass. Creating a small patch of nature in an urban setting has its challenges, but the rewards are enormous. Even the ugliest cinder blocks can be made beautiful with the addition of colorful paint, flowers, shrubs, and trees. In air shafts we can use paint and tangles of vines, such as morning glories, to cover up pipes and ducts.

At one apartment in New York City, we extended the amber-colored dining room by painting the exterior terrace wall a bright orange and planting a variety of flowers with strong colors, such as orange day lilies and hibiscus. On the terrace, the pale, creamy earth tones of the owner's living room extend to the outdoors with a froth of white roses, pale blue verbena, and a mass of Virginia creeper.

If you have a limited amount of space, planting in the foreground as well as in the background, layering colors and shapes, will give an illusion of depth. On a small scale, I will use two window boxes, one inside, the other outside, to create a vivid screen that fluctuates with the wind. Beyond the outside window box, if you can, plant another layer of green.

So many different types of gardens are possible even in the limited space available to us in the city. In one of the four terraces surrounding Robert Redford's New York City apartment, we made a narrow 12-foot-long aromatherapy box filled with thyme, mint, catnip, rosemary, sage, and a variety of hearty perennials. It is not intended as a cooking garden—it exists purely for its beauty and heady scent. On another penthouse terrace we put in a ziggurat of aluminum

Above: Layered terraces frothing with white roses and trumpet vines.

Opposite: On a large, 1,200-square-foot terrace, we created two pavilions: one for dining and one for lounging. In the ziggurat-shaped herb garden, over forty varieties of herbs thrive until they are needed.

177

Garden Varieties

PLAN YOUR GARDEN IN THE SAME WAY THAT YOU WOULD CREATE A FLOOR PLAN FOR A HOUSE. MAKE A DIAGRAM, LIST THE PLANTS THAT YOU LOVE, AND THEN CHECK WITH A GOOD GARDEN BOOK, NURSERY, OR LANDSCAPER TO EXPAND YOUR KNOWLEDGE AND TO ENSURE THAT PLANTS ARE PUT WHERE THEY WILL GROW WELL. MY FAVORITE LANDSCAPER TELLS ME TO OVERPLANT AND LET THE FITTEST SURVIVE. I USE INDIGENOUS PLANTS, KNOWING THAT THEY ARE GOING TO THRIVE, RATHER THAN FORCING IMPORTS FROM OTHER AREAS. EXPERIMENTATION IS GREAT ONCE YOU HAVE A HEALTHY BASE TO WORK FROM. FOR ME, A GARDEN IS A PLACE FOR PLAY, AND THE MAIN GOAL IS TO HAVE FUN THERE.

Generosity is as important to your outdoor landscape as it is inside your home. Here, as in the house, generosity means not just enough, but a bounty. Find a focus for your garden and create a bounteous expression of your idea.

VISUAL LANDSCAPE

- If you want fast gratification from a stand of bamboo in a stone and rock garden or from a field of bluebells, do not skimp on your plantings. A landscape containing many of the same type of flower or plant is a strong presence. Even a humble vinca swarming over a berm can create a sumptuous carpet of leaves starred with ice-blue blossoms.
- Gardens have long been the subject of painting, but paintings can also inform your plantings. Geometric blocks of flowers in primary colors evoke the paintings of Mondrian. A variety of feathery, spiky, and curly greens can remind you of the drawings of van Gogh.

EDIBLE LANDSCAPE

- You might want to enjoy not only looking at your garden but eating it, too. Neat rows of lettuce, radishes, carrots, and arugula can be quite beautiful.
- Plant edible nasturtiums and zucchini on one side of your compost pile. They will flourish there as well as provide a visual shield around the heap of earth.
- Intersperse lavender, rosemary, oregano, and thyme to create a bountiful herbaceous border that will also serve you well in the kitchen.
- Grow scarlet runner beans on the same fence as sweet peas. You can eat one and sniff the other.
- Plant a row of fruit trees or two rows with a path between them. You will enjoy frothy blooms in spring and ripe pears and apples in fall. You can also watch the process of burgeoning and ripening between seasons.
- In the city, plant vegetables or herbs in a window box, or tomato plants in tubs where the vines can climb the railings of the fire escape. The fruits of a small, unexpected edible garden in the city seem as rare and valuable as truffles.

AROMATHERAPY

- An aromatherapy garden can be planted on a terrace or in a sheltered hollow. All you need is a group of fragrant plants like thyme, mint, lavender, lemon geranium, catnip, and sage—to name only a few—growing in profusion.
- On an urban terrace, a long, deep trench can create a barrier of beautiful scent. You can pinch a sprig and inhale deeply or simply sit and let the air transport you to Provence, the Highlands, or wherever else your heart desires. Plant accordingly.
- To find aromatic plants that are pleasing to you, go to a nursery and start sniffing. Some fragrant plants may not have the look you want, so layer them with less fragrant but more appealing-looking plants.

SYMBOLISM

- The garden itself enacts the cycle of birth, life, death, and resurrection.
- Representing the elements and the five human senses is as important in your garden as it is in your home.
- A winding path through different plantings that crosses a bridge over water will bring a meditative aspect to your garden.
- A stone Buddha represents peace.

TIME GARDENS

- In addition to installing a sundial, which in my opinion is the most romantic way of telling the time, a devoted gardener can plot her garden based on the movements of the sun and the seasons.
- Plant a green screen and have various plants and flowers showcase themselves against it through the changing seasons. A maple placed in front of a stand of evergreens will provide a tender light green contrast in spring and become a scarlet haiku in fall.

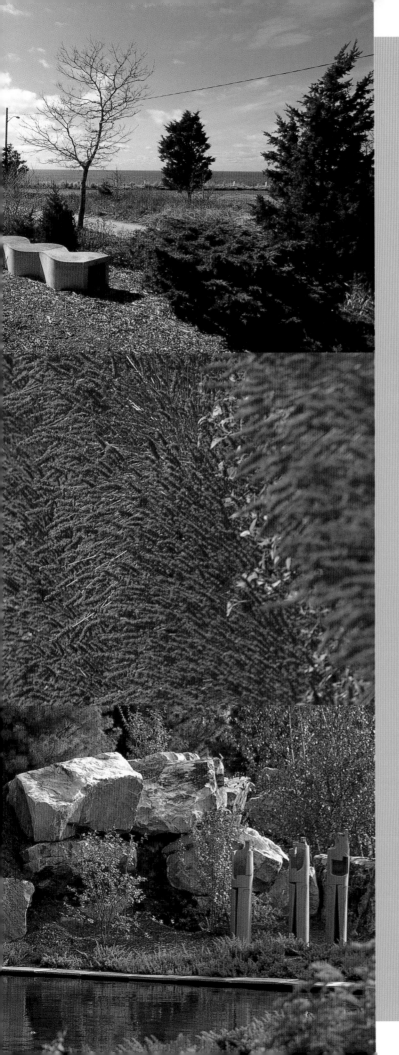

LIGHT AND SHADE

- Place a bench under the dappled shadows of trees.
- A layered, dark cedar tree will pop against a flurry of chartreuse deciduous trees.
- A pergola or a pavilion will throw slatted shadows on a path or terrace.
- At night, totemic outdoor sculptures will cast velvet black moon shadows while white flowers will glimmer like holograms.

WATER GARDENS

- Water is good for the soul. Create a pond by which you can sit and watch shivery dragonflies dip and flit. Plant water lilies, reeds, grasses, stands of purple and gold irises, and wild loosestrife.
- Place a reflecting pool in front of the entrance to your home and have a stone bridge built over it. A walk across water when you return after a long day will change your mood faster than a shot of scotch.
- Install a small motor in the water to create bubbles and ripples. You might want to heat the water slightly so it never freezes.

STILL GARDENS

- Fragments of carefully placed statuary make some of the most beautiful gardens, with the great advantage being that once they are in place, maintenance is negligible.
- Gravel raked around large rocks provides a wonderful still area in which to meditate. A pathway of heavy stepping-stones through a field of gravel provides silence even in a wild cacophony of blooms.

Above: Ornamental grasses, trumpet vines, wisteria, verbenas, and a host of other plants scramble up a tall, woven trellis of wisteria branches, screening out the city views and affording privacy on Robert Redford's Manhattan terrace.

Opposite: The opulence of limestone chenille warms the living room. An antique apricot Oushak rug and mysterious artifacts from the Far East satisfy the owner's sense of wanderlust. A cascade of leafy vines brings soft shadows to a sunlit wall.

boxes in which fifty varieties of herbs grow. The clients can snip herbs for cooking as one would have done in Italy, or simply enjoy the aromatic pleasure of this incredible tangle of herbs twenty-seven stories above ground.

A water garden might serve as a barrier between the peace of your private landscape and the city beyond. The sound of the water, the rustle of grasses, and the peacefulness of the reflecting pool satisfy a longing for nature.

Large gardens afford even more opportunity to apply the philosophy of Total Design. Here you should imagine a series of rooms that reflect the style of the house, with a playroom, an eating area, perhaps a small nook for sipping wine, or a meditative garden with a bench and a fish pond.

At one New England country home we created a series of rooms that begins with an outdoor dining room. The walls are clipped yew and holly trees, and at the center of the terrace sits a massive stone table. On one side is a stacked-stone wall with a waterfall. The wall flows into a barbecue pit made of the same material. Near the house are large terra-cotta pots planted with an herb garden. A steep stone pathway winds through fragrant columbine, spirea, and hydrangea. Ivy and vines wreathe the house. An ancient magnolia embellishes the scene with waxy blossoms in spring.

Permanent sculptural and architectural elements such as freestanding walls and large-scale seating areas further break down the conceptual barriers between indoors and outdoors. At one client's home in California, the central element of the outdoor space is a vast yellow wall with a vertical slot in the center. The wall is a massive outdoor sculpture that separates a play area with a swimming pool and deck on one side and an outdoor dining room with a 13-foot concrete table on the other side. Trees and seasonal plantings soften these three predominant shapes. By combining opposite elements in the right proportions—hard and soft, huge and diminutive, static and changing—you create a discrete world that nourishes and replenishes you.

Gardens exist as much in our minds as in their matter. Every literal fruit has a figurative counterpart. Each root has a history. Each path is the trajectory through time. The ticking of a clock is temporarily replaced by the slow, organic time in seasons measured by risings of the sun. In our hectic lives, the thirst for natural rhythms seems to reach back to before we were born.

Outdoor Rooms

GARDEN ROOMS DEDICATED TO A SPECIFIC, USEFUL FUNCTION WILL GIVE YOU A SENSE OF PURPOSE IN PLANNING AND PLANTING AND WILL DRAW YOU TO SPEND TIME THERE AS YOU WOULD IN THE BEDROOM OR BATHROOM OR LIBRARY INSIDE THE HOME.

BATHING

- Install a hot tub swirling under the stars in the perfume of a night garden fragrant with jasmine and tobacco plants. Place a towel bench nearby and bring out a carafe of lemon water or a glass of wine. In a populated area, a wall of conifers, a living wall of vines, or a low concrete wall will provide privacy.
- Create an outdoor shower adjacent to your house in a place where you can see the stars or the rising sun. I make enclosures of teak, corrugated metal, or masonry.
- A man-made waterfall makes a good shower, especially when coupled with an organic-shaped pool. Create a bench in the pool so you will be able to sit half submerged on a hot summer's day.

COMMON ROOMS

- Outdoor sitting rooms can be as simple as a concrete bench or as complex as a group of teak lounge chairs with side tables, umbrellas, and squishy cushions. The room can be for one or twenty. Define the space with a paved terrace, a sheltering tree, and a good view.
- Add French doors between your kitchen and an outdoor terrace to create an outdoor dining room close to the source of food. Place a massive slab of stone or concrete on a simple base, or buy yourself a big teak outdoor table and install it on a "rug" of stone or tiles.
- A small stone table with two outdoor chairs set close to a south-facing wall will give you a place for intimate evening conversation. Your backs will be warmed by the heat retained by the wall.

MEDITATION

- A water trough with a hammered-copper waterfall conspires to shut out city noise.
- A mossy area with a dip in the center makes a wonderful meditation room. Or you can simply plant bushes and shrubs in a semicircle so your back is protected while you meditate.
- A thick hedge can serve as a sound barrier. If you have the space, create a private room sheltered from the wind and set apart from the rest of the garden.
- A winding or circular footpath of paving stones and moss is good for walking meditation.

NAPPING OR READING

- Placing a bed or just a thick mat in a gazebo will transform it into an outdoor bedroom.
- A hammock slung between two trees invites reading and napping.
- In summer, create a white-columned pavilion looking out over the sea.
- A bed on a terrace garden shaded by a pergola or arched trellis covered with morning glories is a delight each time you visit it.

PLAYING

- If space will allow, an outdoor playroom with a basketball court, a baseball diamond, or nets for goal sports can be set up on one side of the house or in an area some distance removed. Be sure it is far enough away from areas of relaxation so that the loungers are not annoyed by the frolickers.
- Swing sets, slides, seesaws, and tree houses are pleasant additions to a child's outdoor playroom.
- A juniper-green lap pool is both an outdoor exercise room for serious swimmers and an organic pool surrounded by flat rocks for basking in the sun or for conversation and play.
- A field of bluebells under a spring birch is an ideal picnic ground for little children. Add partially sunken tree stumps for a magic circle, using a huge stump as a low table.
- Create a smooth, mossy bank for your kids to roll down, squealing with laughter.

GREEN

SOFT BANKS OF MOSS. SOLDIER ROWS OF ASPARAGUS IN
CHARTREUSE BACKLIT FLUTTER OF SPRING ASPENS. THE
GATSBY WHITE. THE LAYERED VALLEYS OF AN IRISH MORN
PYRAMIDS OF CONIFERS POKING THROUGH SNOW. THE COOL
GREEN SWAMP MIST. THE FORMAL SHEEN OF A MALLARD'S
INTENTION OF ENVIRONMENTALISTS. A PATINATED COPPER
OF AN AMSTERDAM DOOR. MONEY. "GO" ON A TRAFFIC LIGHT
CAL FISH GLINTING AMONG SEA GRASSES. THE FORMALITY
SCRUBS. THE FIRST MIST OF SPRING BUDS. FIGS SPLITTING
OF LETTUCE. MINT'S PUNGENCY AND THE SILVERY FRA
CENT FACE OF A SUMMER PEA.

SPRING. THE VERDANT BOA OF THE NILE'S RIVERBANK. THE
EMERALD VELVET OF A RHODE ISLAND LAWN AGAINST
NG. CARESSING TENDRILS OF A RAIN FOREST CANOPY. TERSE
SUCCULENCE OF AN AVOCADO. HUSKY LODEN. RADIOACTIVE-
HEAD. A STATELY BENCH STANDING IN FALLEN LEAVES. THE
DOME AGAINST A LIGHT GRAY SKY. THE NEARLY BLACK GLOSS
A GLAD PILE OF GRANNY SMITH APPLES. IRIDESCENT TROPI-
OF CARRARA MARBLE. HUNTERS' COATS AND SURGEONS'
WITH THEIR OWN RIPENESS ON TREE BRANCHES. THE HEART
GRANCE OF SAGE. THE FRESH PROMISE OF A LIME. THE INNO-

FANTASY SPACES: SHAPING THE WISH

If you close your eyes and imagine the most perfect room—one that incorporates everything you love, with no thought to viability or budget—you'll have a pretty good idea of what it's like to conceive of a showhouse installation.

The showroom is fleeting. It is part laboratory, part theatrical set, peopled by imaginary occupants who are similar to us but more playful, more indulgent, more flexible than we are. The great luxury of creating one of these temporary installations is that design itself gets pushed to the foreground: there is no need to consider the usual restraints of cost, practicality, or client taste. The room ends up being as close to a pure expression of the designer's vision as you're likely to see.

Do your work as if you had a thousand years to live and as you would if you must die tomorrow.
—Ann Lee, founder of the Shakers

Opposite: A burnished-steel archway leads to a study and anteroom just off the bedroom of this Kips Bay showhouse room. A mirror has been placed over the desk facing the wall so that the person seated at the desk can see who is coming up behind them—a practical attribute of fêng shui. The large glowing ceiling fixture creates a false skylight in a window-less room.

Previous page: The sensual retreat of a four-poster bed is nestled into a niche of indigo plaster. A television is discreetly hidden in the ancient trunk. The bed is draped in fire resistant and easy-care Avora fabrics.

When I begin such a project, I temporarily banish all limits. Ideally, this is the exact path anyone should take when facing redesign of their home or even of one room. The process should be fun, and the best place to start is to let your imagination run wild. There will be plenty of time later for the pragmatic limitations of money or space or the inevitable compromises with cohabitants.

Marcel Proust wrote that "the real voyage of discovery consists not in seeking new lands, but in seeing with new eyes." Like the creation of poetry or music, the design process must begin with total immersion in the unknown. This is followed by an elaborate balancing act in which you suspend preconceptions while still allowing enough of your taste and sense of style to enter in so that the space stays true to you. For me, this means looking to my favorite sources of inspiration—Buddhism, travel, astrology, fêng shui, visual art, ergonomics, and music—and indulging in a healthy amount of hedonism. Each time I design a room for a showhouse I try to reexamine my own prejudices and strip them away. I poke at my ideals to make sure they are sound. I have also learned that if I try to force my own will over the will of the space, the design suffers. At a certain point in the process the very walls and the floors and the mood of a place take over, and I listen to what the space itself is calling for.

In one project, for example, I painted the entryway a sand color, but the rest of the space screamed for something more intense. I had it changed to red immediately. Don't be afraid of making mistakes. The space will tell you what it needs. Basically once you create the structure, it begins to take shape, and certain decisions become inevitable.

Frequently, when I am in the process of working out a room in a private home, the client will insist on keeping a carpet or light fixture that just doesn't belong in the new space. I oblige. But inevitably upon moving in, the client gets rid of the offending piece almost immediately. A space will say yes or no, never maybe, to whatever objects you place in it. The process is somewhat of a mystery to me, but I respect what I don't understand.

When you are attentive to what a space can and cannot support, you will naturally create a harmonious design. When you are designing well, your ego does not interfere. It is a state of openness and respect that I call transparency. When you are transparent you are able to recognize your future self in a space where your life will continue to grow and expand.

(continued on page 197)

192

Love in the Afternoon. This romantic retreat evidences what a little imagination and a lot of work can accomplish. The space was formerly a damp laundry room filled with pipes and vents. We transformed it into a sensuous, Moroccan-inspired lair with a tiny courtyard garden. It is a dreamy cave or an exotic pleasure den, perfect for a late afternoon rendezvous. Air is perfumed with ylang-ylang, jasmine, and olive blossoms. Fragrant tea wafts from an ancient pot.

Eroticism

EROTICISM IS BIGGER THAN SEX. IT ENVELOPS A WIDE RANGE OF SENSUAL PLEASURES, SOLITARY AND SHARED, INVOLVING ALL OF THE SENSES AS WELL AS THE MIND AND THE SPIRIT. IF IT WERE UP TO ME, EACH HOME I DESIGNED WOULD HAVE A ROOM DEDICATED ONLY TO EROTIC PLEASURE, AND EVERY TIME YOU WALKED INTO ONE OF THESE ROOMS YOUR BLOOD WOULD COURSE THROUGH YOUR VEINS. SHORT OF THIS PURITY, WE CAN LOOK AT INCORPORATING ELEMENTS OF THIS IDEAL VISION INTO THE REALITY OF THE LIFE WE REALLY DO LIVE, AND SEE WHAT HAPPENS.

LIGHT Install a love light—a small light on a dimmer switch—that will allow you to unobtrusively set an erotic tone. If you have candles or oil lamps in the room, create a permanent place for matches nearby so that you will actually make use of these items.

AROMA In addition to perfuming the body, perfumed bed sheets, candles, or incense will warm a room and excite the sense of smell. The strong, sweet aroma of certain flowers, such as lilies and roses, is intoxicating. Ylang-ylang is particularly sexy. Musk and spice are classic notes in many perfumes because they evoke an erotic response.

BEDDING Don't economize on bedding—too much of life is spent in bed to deprive yourself. Always get the best-quality sheets and pillows that you can afford. Cotton sheets with a high thread count will feel silky and allow your skin to breathe. Linen gets softer with age and is wonderfully luxurious. Flannels and jersey knit sheets are warm for the winter, but in summer are heavy and clingy. Fine cotton or linen coverlets and a luscious down comforter are staples.

BEYOND THE BED Don't limit yourself to the bedroom: the bath or reading room can be the erotic center of the house and so can a well-protected outdoor space. If your erotic life takes place in various parts of the house, make sure that the window treatments provide privacy and that the doors and walls are properly insulated so you can remain in the moment.

THE SECRET DRAWER Work into your design a place to store toys, potions, and condoms. Mystery is titillating—an individual lockable drawer for each partner may feed curiosity.

MEDIA Place a television in the appropriate room if you like to watch erotic films. If music is very pleasurable to you, consider installing a small selection of tapes or CDs and the necessary machinery. Situate the controls for these devices in easy-to-reach places. The fewer obstacles there are, the happier you will ultimately be.

REFLECTION A reflective surface can be subtly erotic, whether it is a mirror lining a door that can be opened at a certain angle, or a polished lacquer surface that hints at but does not fully reveal your image.

Not of the letter but of the spirit.
—*II Corinthians 3:6*

(continued from page 190)

Pictured in this chapter are showroom spaces I designed over several years for the Kips Bay Boys and Girls Club Decorator Showhouse in New York City. The main purpose of these spaces is to inspire. They are a retreat to a nearby reality, where designers and spectators can envision themselves in a rarefied state. In the way that haute couture informs ready-to-wear, these highly designed interiors created with huge budgets establish an attitude toward interior space that can be adapted for smaller projects in your own home.

A ROOM OF ONE'S OWN

There is a lot packed into the intimate space pictured opposite. I wanted to create a room where you could spend an entire weekend and not run out of things to do, a beautiful, harmonious room you wouldn't want to leave. The result is a common room with many smaller rooms held inside: a cross between a family room and a trysting spot; a room in which to be on one's own to read and think and meditate; a playroom with a lot of different stations in which friends can engage one another.

I brought a great deal of personal nostalgia to bear in this room. A photographic collage triggers a stream of memories of life with children, friends, and family and is sandwiched between 5-by-4-foot sheets of glass; an alcove is lined with shelves of books and memorabilia. Many of the patterns and shapes and colors in the room were inspired by my travels in Africa: a tall screen that evokes Masai shields leaning against a hut, the black pattern on the pale carpet, and the vibrant fabric on various chairs. A tented corridor leads to a meditation niche where Buddha sits on a stone in a reflecting pool. Behind the Buddha, water splashes softly in a glass fountain.

It is a small room, but it continues to grow. A room-expanding mirror hangs over the fireplace in the main room. The seating configurations invite movement: a high-backed sofa for conversation, a chair and ottoman for solitary reading, two tall-backed chairs with a backgammon table between them near a window.

CHAMBER MUSIC

The red-lacquered entryway and dropped ceilings give you the feeling of crossing a bridge into something special, something exotic. This space is about the past, the present, and the future.

In the main room, a massive bed is nestled into its own indigo blue room-

Opposite: In a corridor niche plastered the color of Burmese red lacquer, a Buddha sits amid papyrus and water and waits for the day's moment of meditation. A ritual candle focuses the mind.

Overleaf: Fabrics by Trevira inspired the fantasy pavilion we created for a trade fair in Brussels. Because it was situated in the midst of a busy show, the pavilion was needed to offer a respite from the heavy traffic all around and celebrate the senses and the elements. In the center, a fifteen-foot-high corrugated fiberglass waterfall splashed into a reflecting pool surrounded by mattress-quilted cushions where visitors could relax for a moment of quiet. Evocative fragrance, a soundtrack orchestrated by Peter O'Kennedy that encompassed the distant sound of a train, the clop of horses' hooves, the haunting strains of a Chopin piano concerto, and the faint trill of birdsong, reinforce the contemplative mood. Fluttering in the breezes of summer fans, fire-resistant textiles by Trevira drape both sides of the pavilion, illustrating that beauty and safety can walk hand in hand.

Above: The archway of the niche housing this four-poster romantic hideaway was lowered to emphasize the ceiling height of the main room.

Opposite: A slate-colored, cast-concrete mantel is topped with a mirrored chimney.

200

within-a-room. To lie in the bed is to sink down into your own private, meditative world. You can imagine you are anywhere. The bed is very primitive-looking, inspired by palm tree trunks. A swish of metallic blue drapery hangs over the tall banisters.

From the bed the eye is drawn to the main room where an earthy Chinese "water rug" replaced a brightly colored carpet, which the space rejected. This rare antique rug is appropriate here, balancing centuries of change: futuristic steel trays holding brilliant green grass by the window, an antique trunk at the foot of the bed, a comfortable dark blue chair for reading, a red ottoman that doubles as a table. The fireplace warms the room both visually and literally.

This space is a world unto itself, an intersection of many worlds. There is no need to leave; everything is here. There is a home office in one small adjoining room for contact with the outside world. There is a Zen bathing room. Yearning for the sense of freedom that I experienced when bathing outdoors in Africa, I re-created the experience in another adjoining room where a fantastic chiseled concrete tub sits in the glory of light streaming like the sun through a slotted ceiling. The atmosphere is magical and cleansing in all respects.

More than the others, this space was very demanding: it knew what it was to be. I just had to figure it out.

In the average household it is not always feasible to undertake a massive redesign along the lines of these fantasy spaces. There are usually constraints of space, time, and money. But introducing even a single clear gesture or element into a room can redirect the whole space. You can resurface an appliance in your kitchen. You can buy a selection of aromatherapy candles to give each room in the house a different scent. You can keep a vase in the entryway stocked with fresh flowers. You can sell off all the things that no longer work for you and buy one piece of furniture that you love.

The rooms pictured here realize visions and dreams that are mine. My hope is that they express a purity of intention that can be translated by you, the observer, and added to your own lexicon. The elements can shift, flip, or turn inside out and over. And when the limits must finally be attended to, the real work is to achieve a balance—between what can be imagined and what can be achieved, between the outer life and the inner one, between the comfort that the body needs and the space craved by the soul.

ESOTERICA

Layers of lime wash peel away history and reveal a taste of past decades. A scribble of blue rope, interesting rust, and weathered timber can inspire an entire color story. Massive, sliding copper doors close off the room to contain a hidden, secret world. Layering similar colors and metals gives depth and sensuality to the space. A custom-designed door-pull greets each visitor with a warm welcome.

BLACK

NIGHT SHADOWS CAST BY THE MOON. THE EBONY RIPPLE O
TECH INTIMIDATION. AN EBONY BENCH FROM ZAMBIA. A PAR
GRAPHIC LOCUS OF GESTURE AND MEANING. THE BOTTON
NECKLACE ON A PALE THROAT. THE FRIENDLY SEED OF A
VICTORIAN MOURNING LACE. THE INVITATION OF A BLACK
SUMMER ROAD. A WET LABRADOR RETRIEVER SHAKING OF
LETS. AN IRON FENCE ENCLOSING A PALACE. THE STEEL
CHARCOAL SCRATCHING ON WHITE CANVAS. A GLIMPSE O
IN SNOWBOUND BRUGES. YEWS AT TWILIGHT. A SAUNTER O
A SHINED SHOE. A WITCH'S HAT.

A STALLION'S MANE. THE WARM PROMISE OF CORAL. A HIGH-
ROT'S BEAK. AN UNLIT TUNNEL. NIGHT MUSIC. A CALLI-
OF AN INKWELL. TRANSLUCENT BEADS OF CAVIAR. AN ONYX
LYCHEE NUT. A CROW ON A SUCCULENT GREEN SPRING LAWN.
BOARD. A SQUID'S INK JET. THE PUNGENCY OF PITCH ON A
AN AURA OF DIAMOND DROPS. RACKS OF CAST-IRON SKIL-
STALK OF A CAT. THE DEFINITION OF A DALMATIAN'S SPOTS.
THE SOUL THROUGH THE PUPIL OF AN EYE. WINTER CANALS
JACKDAWS THREATENING A CHIMNEY. THE STRICT SHEEN OF

BLUE

THE INFINITY OF LAVENDER FIELDS IN PROVENCE. THAT
MEDITERRANEAN AFTERNOON. AQUA DEPTHS OF TH
DWELLING FLOWERS OF CHILDHOOD: SPEEDWELL, PERIWIN
OF THE FIRST SPRING VIOLET. MILES DAVIS'S JAZZ REFLEC
OF A BLUEJAY FLASHING ACROSS LOCUST TREES. THE IRI
SURFACE. THE WISDOM OF A SAGE BLOSSOM. MIDNIGHT
SION OF A LONG-RANGE FLIGHT ON A CLEAR DAY. SMOKY
AURA OF LOST LOVE. AN INDIGO CUP IN KYOTO. THE MILITANT
CONCORD GRAPES. THE PROMISE OF BLUEPRINTS. THE
KNEE. THE CLEAR GAZE OF A BABY. CRACKLED CHINESE
QUICK HISS OF A WINTER FLAME. THE CARESS OF BLUE VELVET

MOMENT WHEN THE SKY MERGES WITH THE SEA ON A CARIBBEAN FRILLED WITH WHITE SURF. THE GROUND-KLE, GRAPE HYACINTH, CHIONODOXA. THE SHY APPEARANCE TIONS. FIRST PRIZE IN THE PONY SHOW. THE HARSH HAIKU DESCENT MACKEREL FLASHING JUST BELOW THE OCEAN'S DEPTHS OF THE SANTA FE SKY. THE LOST-IN-SPACE SUSPEN-LIGHT IN A BLUES LOUNGE. THE HARD STARE OF SLATE. AN BRAVERY OF AN IRIS. THE VEILED SHEEN OF BLUEBERRIES AND YOUNGISH EASE OF DENIM. A TENDER BRUISE ON A CHILD'S PORCELAIN. A RIPPLING LAKE OF SPRING BLUEBELLS. THE SNOW SHADOWS.

Workbook

TURNING DESIGN IDEAS INTO PHYSICAL REALITY CAN BE A DAUNTING PROCESS. IT IS HARD TO KNOW WHERE TO START AND HOW TO PROCEED. THIS WORKBOOK IS MODELED ON THE SURVEYS I COMPLETE WITH MY CLIENTS. IT IS ESSENTIALLY A SERIES OF QUESTIONS AND RELEVANT OBSERVATIONS TO HELP YOU BETTER ARTICULATE YOUR IDEAS AND NEEDS AND DEFINE YOUR DESIGN GOALS.

The space you are creating should be completely specific to who you are. For that reason, you will find the questions that follow are very personal. Your responses will amount to a blueprint of your past and your desires for the future, your living habits, and a catalog of frustrations with your current space. This is the time to fantasize. Don't temper your responses as you work through these pages. There will be plenty of opportunities later in the process to construct a budget and figure out alternative solutions if money and space become constraining.

Photocopy this section of the book and make enough copies for each person in your household. Be sure to read through these pages within a limited time frame, preferably in one sitting, as our first gut responses are often the surest. Do not try to influence each other at this point. This is not a competition or a territorial invasion; it is a tool for collecting and organizing facts that will help you work toward realizing your goals for the design or redesign of your home. It will be helpful if you highlight whatever is especially important to you; that way you can more easily communicate the negotiable and nonnegotiable points later on.

In a notebook or ring binder with a separate page devoted to each room or space, compile the responses of each person in your household. Leave space for general notes describing shared and individual likes and dislikes. At this point your project should exist only as words without images, because language leaves you the freedom to explore. After you have made the lists, you can begin to assemble samples, colors, and photographs that represent your ideas. If you are working with a designer or architect, this workbook will help you show him or her what you want. If you are on your own, it will help keep you focused and serve as a useful reference if you become mired in the process.

Before you begin responding to the questions, put yourself in a quiet place both physically and mentally. Disconnect the phone, if possible, so that you can examine your thoughts undisturbed.

THE FIRST STEP

Whether you are building a new home or redesigning an existing space, the design process starts with the basic question: Who lives here, and how do these individuals spend their time? In other words, what kinds of lives will these spaces house and nurture? The number of required rooms, their necessary functions and specific features, and the kinds of changes or additions you desire will flow logically and effortlessly from your well-considered answers.

• Look ahead to the foreseeable future. If you are single, do you prefer the single life or hope one day to have a live-in partner or children? If you are married, is there a baby on the way, or is this soon to be your "empty nest"?

• Is this your primary residence? A weekend home? A professional office as well as a home? Are household help or other workers—or colleagues, or clients—in and out every day? Is this your first home or your retirement home? Multilevel homes with lots of stairs are less than ideal for the very young or the very old.

• Who visits you, and how do you entertain? If you have young children, do they love having sleepovers? Do grown children come home for holidays and vacations? Alone, or with friends or mates? Are grandchildren in the picture? Or will an elderly parent move in someday? Do you have live-in nannies or nurses, or anticipate a future need? Do you love to host lavish parties and salons? Are a barbecue and a card game with your buddies more your style? Or is a quiet candlelight dinner *a deux* your idea of the perfect night in?

• Do you have pets?

• Who sleeps in your house? Who eats there? Who cooks? Who works in it? Who has hobbies? Is equipment involved? Is a dedicated space required? A darkroom? A greenhouse? A tool shop? A studio for writing, painting, sculpting, or recording? Are there bicycles, skis, skates? Musical instruments? Is there art or collectibles to be displayed?

Make a list of all the kinds of things, large and small, that you do—or would like to do—in your home. Look it over as you begin to imagine and consider the many possible uses for your space. Then, consider how many rooms you require in order to accommodate the various members of your household and their particular interests and needs:

• How many rooms do you need?

• How many cars will your garage have to house?

• What size kitchen do you need? Do you want to eat there? Is it largely for plating takeout and preparing light meals, or are you a serious cook who needs professional equipment and a separate pantry?

• How many bedrooms do you need? Do you want separate dressing rooms?

• How much space will you dedicate to houseguests? Space constraints may decide for you whether you can house guests in their own rooms, or in a multifunctional room.

• How many bathrooms do you need? Are the present ones well located?

• Are there rooms that you would like to join by breaking down a nonsupporting wall? Consider opening up the kitchen and dining room or making two small bedrooms into one larger room. Do you want a separate formal living room, or would it be better to have a family room, kitchen, and dining room combined into one?

• Are there rooms you would like to divide with a partition? A partial wall in a large bedroom, for example, protects the privacy of the sleeping area and creates a dressing room.

• Do you need separate work spaces for different members of the household? Can the workspaces be located inside of a larger room, or do they have to be self-contained? A message and communication center set off in a nook can simplify your life and hold fax machines or home photocopiers that might otherwise disturb the look of a room.

• Do you need a nursery or a separate playroom for children? (Anyone who has had to wade through a carpet of toys to get to the kitchen may think so.) Children's bedrooms can be small, but playrooms should be designed so that they can be used for modeling clay and painting, and they should provide enough room to jump around and have fun.

• If you have pets, are they housesitters or backyard adventurers? Do they require a fence, a cage, a doghouse, a barn? Do you want a place to groom and feed them and to store their supplies, litter box, or crate? If you have an aquarium, plan to locate it where it can be enjoyed all the time.

• Make a note of any other special rooms you may want, such as a sauna or steam shower; a painting, writing, or music studio; a separate room for exercising; a room for audiovisual and media equipment; a special area to lay out clothes for travel and a suitcase for packing; a laundry room and linen storage closet; or a curatorial closet where you can keep items such as artwork and seasonal decorations.

Use the following Room-by-Room Checklist as a guide to

210

ROOM-BY-ROOM CHECKLIST

Transitional Spaces
- ❑ Driveway/Walkway
- ❑ Garage
- ❑ Exterior Entrance(s)
- ❑ Interior Mud Room
- ❑ Foyer
- ❑ Stairway/Landings
- ❑ Hallway(s)
- ❑ Interior Loft/Balcony

Kitchen and Common Rooms
- ❑ Kitchen
- ❑ Message Center/Office
- ❑ Pantry
- ❑ Wet Bar/Kitchenette
- ❑ Breakfast Room
- ❑ Dining Room
- ❑ Family Room/Den
- ❑ Living Room
- ❑ Other

Master Suite
- ❑ Bedroom
- ❑ Bathroom
- ❑ Dressing Rooms
- ❑ Sitting Room
- ❑ Other

Children's Suite
- ❑ Nursery
- ❑ Bedroom(s)
- ❑ Bathroom
- ❑ Playroom/Study
- ❑ Other

Guest/Spare Rooms
- ❑ Powder Room
- ❑ Bedroom

- ❑ Bathroom
- ❑ Au Pair Bedroom
- ❑ Au Pair Bathroom
- ❑ Staff Rooms/Suite
- ❑ Other

Dedicated Rooms
- ❑ Media/Music Room
- ❑ Library/Study
- ❑ Office/Study
- ❑ Studio/Hobbyroom
- ❑ Game Room
- ❑ Exercise/Spa Room
- ❑ Meditation Room
- ❑ Sun Room/Atrium
- ❑ Other

Utility/Storage Rooms
- ❑ Laundry Room
- ❑ Tool//Hobbyshop
- ❑ Wine Cellar
- ❑ Boiler Room
- ❑ Basement/Storage
- ❑ Attic/Storage
- ❑ Walk-In/Cedar Closet
- ❑ Other

Exterior Rooms
- ❑ Terrace/Deck
- ❑ Patio
- ❑ Sun Porch
- ❑ Summer Kitchen/Barbecue
- ❑ Pool/Deck
- ❑ Cabana/Guest House
- ❑ Outdoor Shower
- ❑ Equipment/Tool Shed
- ❑ Tennis Court/Other
- ❑ Gardens
- ❑ Other

help you narrow down the exact number and choice of rooms you hope to have in your new home, ticking off the ones you plan to design. The completed form is a simple blueprint of your project—the basic sketch of your new home in a few words. Then create a separate page for each of the rooms

THE ROOMS OF YOUR HOME

Now, begin to focus on the specific spaces of your home and the fine details of their design.

Transitional Spaces

Entrances, foyers, hallways, and stairways are the passageways into and through our homes. The entryway is the point of identity. It provides our first impression and our first line of defense. We spend only fleeting moments in these spaces as we come and go, making it all the more important to design them to be efficient and to enhance the flow of positive energy through our environment.

• Do you live in a private home? Can the house number be readily seen from the street? Do guests have an attractive and welcoming access to your front door? Think of your property as an integral part of your home's overall design. Consider the juxtaposition of its natural and man-made elements—stone, wood, metal, water, plantings. Do they work together and contribute to the overall impression? Does the design flow easily? Is it pleasant to walk through? Well lit?

• If you live in an apartment, do you have a voice in the design of the building entry and hallways? Or the ability to make changes in the foyer immediately outside your door?

• Is there a handy drop point in your home entryway for keys, purse, umbrellas, etc.? A coatrack or closet? A close-by mirror for last-minute beauty checks? Are switches conveniently located for both interior and exterior lights?

• Do you need a back entrance or mud room? Do you have a shoes-off household? If so, is there a bench for removing and storing footwear?

• How big does the main closet need to be? The climate in which you live will determine some of your requirements. A South Florida beachfront home might not need a large coat closet, but an outdoor shower or hose to wash off sandy feet would be convenient, as would an entrance directly from pool deck to bathroom.

• Once inside, what is the first thing you see? What impression does the foyer convey about your home? Consider all the elements: lighting, color, wall treatments, floor coverings, furnishings, and artwork. Distinctive architectural features can add drama—consider a balcony, a grand stairway, a wall of windows.

Kitchens and Dining Rooms

Although the kitchen and dining areas are common rooms, I treat them separately in the survey because their many functions—cooking, serving, eating, cleaning, celebrating, and so forth—are not only site specific and often labor intensive, they also play a central part in our daily lives.

A functional, beautiful, bountiful kitchen is a Mecca where the hungry gather to feed body and soul. More than any other room, it is a temple of sensuality. Where else do we indulge ourselves in hedonistic pleasures—the succulence of a ripe red plum, the pungency of garlic, the comforting warmth of oven-fresh bread, the sight of a feast spread out on a table, the reassuring sound of clattering plates and conversation? Here are some questions to get you thinking about what you want from your kichen:

• What sort of look will your kitchen have: rustic American, French country, high-tech, or a whimsical mix of styles. Keep in mind that kitchens demand more functionality than other rooms, and good ergonomics apply to any style. Personally, I like a kitchen that is totally stripped, like a blank theater set, so that when I come from the market I can pile white eggplants or peaches in beautiful bowls and feast with my eyes while preparing a meal.

• Make a list of appliances, hand tools, and cookware that you cannot live without, and buy the best you can afford. Choose a few excellent items and avoid cluttering your kitchen with gadgets. Be sure to factor in enough storage for all your equipment. If you have room, consider a separate pantry.

• Is there more than one chef in your household? If so, multiple full-cooking areas are ideal. Even if you have just a few feet of counter space, divide it down the middle so each person has a work area, for collision-free, friction-free sharing. A knife drawer between two small workstations is better than a knife drawer at one end of a longer workstation. If you have a tiny kitchen, buy a folding cart or restaurant supply cart. Use the top as a chopping board and put storage underneath.

• Most of us love counter space. Measure out what you really need, allotting an extra counter near the cooktop for pots and pans, as well as a place to stack dishes. If you are tight for counter space, consider an under-counter or upper-cabinet refrigerator with a separate under-counter freezer instead of a standard refrigerator.

• Is your counter height best at the standard 36 inches or at 38 inches? Stack two cutting boards on your existing counter to see if that height seems more comfortable. Fêng shui master Sarah Rossbach advises mirroring your backsplash so that people cannot come up behind you unexpectedly. (If the splash runs over the stove, use mirror-polished stainless steel—the heat will crack a mirror.) Install more lighting than you think you need. You will be grateful when it comes to chopping and cleaning up.

• For sinks, I always suggest two: a deep one and a shallow one. You will find each is useful for different tasks. Consider a water filter to provide pure water inexpensively from the tap for cooking and drinking.

• Are you a righty or a lefty? Install the dishwasher to your right if you are right handed and vice versa if you are left handed. (If there is a lefty and a righty in the family, install the dishwasher to the right, as lefties are more used to adjusting.)

• Do you want four burners or six? How about a grill? A vent for high-volume stovetop cooking? Does the cooktop need to be attached to the oven, or does it make more sense in your kitchen to install a wall oven so that you can use the area under the cooktop for storage? How many ovens do you need? If you like to host big parties, consider double ovens in addition to a microwave.

• Do you like to cook food ahead of time? Consider an under-counter additional freezer or a large freezer in the pantry. If you are a vegetarian, and fill the fridge quickly with produce, consider a side-by-side refrigerator/freezer or a separate under-counter refrigerated produce drawer to give yourself more space.

• Well-designed cabinets, drawers, and storage are the key to an efficient, easy-to-use kitchen. Pull-out pantries with double-sided storage and six-inch-deep shelving are excellent for glasses, spices, oils, vinegars, teas, cans, and other small food items, which are too easily lost in the back of deeper cabinets. Use drawer dividers to keep small hand tools separate and accessible. Do you prefer a pot rack or drawers for your cookware? Try to store pots and lids together for easy access. Do you prefer to keep small appliances out on the counter or concealed in an easy-to-open appliance garage?

• For convenience, keep garbage cans and a compost bucket near your food preparation area. Consider a full-height, under-the-counter drawer with two bins, one for wet waste, the second for paper and other recyclables.

• What amenities do you want in the kitchen? A phone? A sound system? A TV? To avoid the dangers of tangled or melting cords, use a cordless telephone (a headset lets you cook and chat simultaneously), and keep the base out of the way in a cabinet. Consider hooking a small TV onto a pole or bracket so that you can practice your cooking technique along with the experts on Food Network.

• Do you like to write or do take-home work in the kitchen? You can easily create a small computer ledge or even a tiny home office in one corner.

• If you have pets, a dedicated pet area works well here; store litter, food, brushes, and other supplies in the pantry.

• Do you want an eating area in the kitchen, adjoining it, or separated from it completely? Do you want a breakfast table or room? An eating counter with stools can serve double duty as a youngster's homework station, allowing you to help with assignments and still get meals on the table.

• What style of dining do you prefer for everyday? For special guests? For family occasions? Casual or formal? Do you like small gatherings, or do you need an extension table that holds service for twelve? If so, consider where to store the leaves. Note: The optimal height for a dining table is 28 to 29 inches.

• In your main dining area, what type of environment do you want to create? Do you want a sleek, utilitarian look with little more than a long steel table and an oversized canvas on the wall? Do you want French doors to a dining patio? A fireplace? Bookshelves? Combining the library and dining room is an excellent choice because it enhances the functions of both. The dining table provides the perfect surface for research and writing, while books lend an air of intimacy and warmth to the dining experience.

• Do you have enough seating in your dining area for every family member and enough spare seating for guests? Keep extra chairs in other nearby rooms. If there are youngsters in the picture, an antique high chair is both practical and decorative. Consider two tables: one adult size, one kid size.

• Arrange for each seat location to have a pleasant view—a window, a breakfront, a wall hanging, a piece of artwork.

• Do you prefer to display your dinnerware in a hutch or glass-fronted cabinet or to conceal it behind cupboard doors? If you own beautiful china or art plates, why keep them hidden away just for special occasions?

• Is there a nearby buffet or server? Make sure the surface is sealed or protected to withstand hot, cold, and spills—ditto for the dining table.

• Proper lighting can make or break a dining experience. Direct illumination over the table is best. Use dimmer switches and candles to set the mood.

• Make sure the centerpiece or table decor is not obtrusive, allowing for easy conversation and eye contact.

• Select a floor covering that works visually and practically. Consider potential problems of sliding chairs (snag on carpeting) and the occasional spill.

• What other eating spaces would you like in your home? A café table and two chairs tucked under a living-room window view? A casual table in the family room for serving snacks and TV dinners to the kids—and for playing cards at night? A picnic table on a patio or terrace?

Common Rooms

A common room should be a joyful gathering place for family and friends. As the locus of household activity, it is necessarily a flexible room and, especially if you have children at home, a casual room. The questions on pages 209 to 210 will help you to reach the necessary consensus about which shared interests the common room should serve. Keep in mind that some activities do not mix well in a single space. A piano in the common room is perfect for a household of musicians, but not for a family of couch potatoes, particularly if your budding Horowitz practices during primetime.

• In my view, the common room must include an open kitchen; otherwise, the person at the stove feels exiled while everyone else is having fun without him or her. Swivel-based armchairs and counter stools give a 360-degree view of the room, so you can enjoy the scenery and conversation in any direction.

• Are children welcome in the room? If so, adequate storage is a must. Make sure there is a place for everything or it will look forever like you just moved in. A big closet or armoire gives kids easy access to their toys and gives you a convenient place to hide the clutter. An antique trunk or wooden chest can serve double duty as toy box and coffee table. Special playthings like a painted rocking horse, a beautiful doll, a giant stuffed bear, a miniature tea set, or a model train are perfect for a common room because they never have to be put away. Don't forget storage for adult playthings, too, such as camcorders, cameras, and the card table and chairs for weekly card games.

• For versatility, a luxurious easy-care area rug on a wood or tiled floor beats wall-to-wall carpeting any day of the week. You can sit on it comfortably with your toddler all morning, then roll it up to party all night.

• Does your family hang out to watch TV? Two monitors and remote headsets enable Mickey Mouse and CNN to coexist peacefully in one room.

- The common room is the center of action and a good place to put the liquor cabinet and bar. Why leave the room to pour wine or mix a cocktail if family and guests are all here?
- What kind of seating do you plan—sofas, sectionals, big overstuffed chairs with ottomans? A three-section sofa is conversational and ideal for lounging (make sure it's long enough so you can stretch out head to toe); two sections provide intimacy. For sitting, make sure the sofa seat is not too high. Try it out before you bring it home.
- Do you have an outdoor garden or terrace? The area closest to the common room is the ideal place to have al fresco dining and barbecues. If possible, put a pass-through in an adjacent kitchen wall for easy serving and, directly underneath, an outdoor table of stone or concrete built into the wall.

Sleeping and Waking

- Is the bedroom for one, or will it be shared? If shared, do you and your partner keep different schedules? Note who gets up early or late. Make a list of noisome activities that typically awaken you, such as exercise, grinding coffee, or the general rustle of someone else's morning grooming rituals. Plan to separate those activities from the sleeping area, either by soundproofing or lightproofing, or by placing them in another room altogether. You might also investigate remote earphones so that you can exercise and watch television in a small space without disturbing your partner.
- Do you read in bed until the early hours? If so, your reading light should be carefully chosen so as not to spill light over to where your partner is sleeping.
- Do you need blackout shades in your bedroom? Some people cannot sleep when daylight comes into the room. And sometimes a streetlight will shine into your window, casting an orange glow over your sleep for the whole night. A blackout shade will let you reach a deeper state of sleep.
- Do you sleep with pajamas, in a T-shirt, or in the nude? Your habits may determine the type of window coverings you select.
- Is one of you a restless sleeper? If so, do you need a second bed somewhere for particularly restless nights?
- Do you want sleeping space for guests? In a separate room, or a multifunctional room? If you have space for a spare guestroom, stock it with the kinds of amenities that welcome travelers in fine hotels. Do you have need for a spare bedroom suite, perhaps for a nanny or other household help? Or for visiting in-laws or children?

Dressing

- Do you want a dressing room that is separate from your bedroom?
- Do you travel to locations with different extremes of climate and therefore need to keep winter and summer clothes available at all times? I endorse the personal boutique idea for clothing storage. By this I mean that you should keep clothing for all seasons together and hang them in color groupings (the only items I put into storage elsewhere are heavy winter coats and wool sweaters in summer).
- Do you need hooks so that you can undress and hang your clothes for the night before checking them and putting them away the next day? Or do you like to choose your clothes for the following morning and leave them ready for a fast exit?
- Note the number of hangers you will need. For visual appeal, hangers should match and skirts should be hung with clips. There are special hangers with many hooks to store ties and belts.
- Do you like separate cubes for storing heavy sweaters and folded items, or do you like them on shelves?
- Take stock of your current drawer space. If you do not have to squeeze things in, or leave things stacked around the dresser, you have enough. If not, note how much more space you need and for what kinds of storage. Separate compartmentalized drawers work well for underwear, stockings, socks, and small items, such as jewelry storage, change, watch, wallet, or tie clip. Shallow drawers often work better than deep ones. If you stack things in a deep drawer, you mess up things each time you take out the bottom item. I size my drawers by content and make dividers for the smaller things so that they do not all jam together when I close the drawers in a hurry.
- Do you store your shoes on shelves or on racks? Count the pairs of shoes you need to store and measure the linear feet required.
- Do you prefer sliding doors that reveal the closet partially or doors that can open wide, giving you a full frontal view?
- Have you thought about a long mirror? Do you want to see yourself from the back? Two doors can be mirrored inside to achieve this effect.

Bathing and Grooming

The bathroom is a place to explore sensuality: Put on your favorite music, light scented candles, install a good reading light. A waterfall or fountain lets you enjoy the full water experience, sounds and all, even after you've stopped running the bath.

- When I design a bathroom, I separate functions where possible. Can you tuck toilets and bidets behind half walls or sandblasted glass enclosures and place the items for more social activities, such as bathing and showering, in spots where you can relax and talk to a friend, lover, or spouse?
- Do you need storage underneath your wash basin sink?
- If you have small children, make sure you have a step stool, child-safety locks on under-counter cabinets and medicines, hair dryers and other small electrical appliances securely out of reach. Do you have room for rubber ducks, whimsical toothbrushes, a shelf for some books, a waterproof chair you can

pull up to the tub? When my children were little, the nightly rituals of the bath included stories and sharing of the day.

• What sorts of accessories do you like in the bathroom? Hooks for terry robes? Heated towel bars? Racks for spare towels? Surfaces on which to put things down? In the guest bath, provide extra storage space, towel racks, and travel-size bath accessories.

• Mirrors are important for good grooming. What sizes do you want, and where will they hang? You should have good lights on either side of your mirror for makeup application, shaving, and tweezing. A magnifying mirror, though terrifying at first, will help you to keep your makeup straight.

• If you spend a lot of time in the tub, install lights on a dimmer switch, and make sure you face something beautiful when you are lying in your tub. Wherever you look, you should see something pleasurable. If you don't have a view, place a damp-resistant piece of art there.

• If you read in the bath, install a magazine rack.

• Do you need an area to store and apply your makeup?

• If there is room for each person to have a personal medicine cabinet, I recommend it. If not, dedicate a shelf within a shared cabinet to each person using it.

• If you like to listen to music while bathing or showering and getting ready for the day, consider putting speakers in the ceiling.

• Consider radiant heat in your floor to warm cold tiles on chilly mornings.

• Is there adequate ventilation?

Children's Rooms

Ask your children to prepare wish lists for their own bedrooms, study, and playroom. Help them sketch them out. Ask them their favorite colors, textures, and shapes as well as their most beloved books and characters. Get their ideas *first*. It's fun to plan and very revealing. Let them take charge of their rooms' design and appearance, and you keep charge of organizing them, providing safety and security, and giving your kids lots of love and opportunity to grow—not only in their personal spaces but throughout the home. Then consider the following:

• Does your child's room have adequate, easy-access storage for toys, clothes, books, etc.? Are there kid-size tables and chairs, at which they can comfortably eat and play? Do you have at least one large low-to-the-ground surface (approximately coffee-table height) to hold and display toy sets, such as Playmobil or other miniature toys, dollhouses, Erector sets, and train tracks?

• Is there space for a separate playroom? How about a dress-up room with lots of mirrors and a trunk for the clothes? An extra walk-in closet or an unused corner of the attic or basement will do. Give the kids your hand-me-downs—mom's party dresses, high heels, and rhinestone jewels; dad's suits,

ties, overalls, and hats; and plenty of miscellaneous items for creating costumes and characters. Add an extra curtain and the dress-up room becomes a stage.

• Are you planning for a new baby? Is the nursery close to your bedroom and a bathroom? Do you have an adequate waste can for disposable diapers and a hamper for soiled clothes? Do you have a rocking chair and daybed nearby for midnight feedings?

• Do you have a portable phone that works in every room, including the bathroom, so that you never have to leave your child to take or place calls, especially in emergencies?

• If you have small children at home, decide which spaces should be child friendly and which childproof. If you keep a step stool for them in the bathroom or kitchen, make sure drugs, chemicals, and sharp items are well out of reach or properly secured. Cover any sharp corners on counters or glass tabletops. Also install nonskid surfaces in showers and tubs and nonskid mats under rugs; safety bars and fire safety labels on all windows; electrical outlet covers; and child-safety locks on low cabinets, especially those housing household products, garbage, electrical appliances, or precious breakables.

Dedicated Rooms

A room dedicated solely to an activity you enjoy offers many advantages. Chief among them is that you can hide yourself, and your task, away from the household behind a closed door. If you don't have the luxury of a spare room, there are still creative ways to establish a dedicated space for your work or your passions within another room.

The home office is a common choice for a dedicated room (see page 136), but there are many other pursuits besides work that may warrant a space apart from your usual domestic activities. Let your personal passions be your guide in this decision and let the function of the room dictate its design. Keep the environment clean and spare. Let the space itself tell the story of what goes on there. In a music room, a grand piano, or a cello beside a scrolled music stand, easily takes center stage with its understated beauty. A book-lined room needs no introduction. A meditation room is recognizable by all that it is empty of—a few large pillows stacked on the floor, a yoga mat, a table for candles and incense, perhaps a small personal altar, and the room is complete. Too many extraneous objects, no matter how lovely in their own right, distract from the purpose or pleasure at hand.

To dedicate is to set apart, or to consecrate. Honor the integrity of this special place in your home. Whether it is dedicated to your work or your play, make it a personal sanctuary.

• What kind of activity do you want to accommodate? Is your passion reading, sewing, painting, playing pool, working out, building model boats? Do you want a private study or office, a place to talk on the phone, work on the computer, research and write, or spread out your papers? Do you want a darkroom or a studio to paint, sculpt, or throw pots? Some of these activities may require a larger space and additional plumbing or electrical wiring.

• Describe what you need in terms of storage and equipment. Do you need a computer, scanner, printer, phone, fax, copier, drafting table, filing cabinets, shelves, book shelves, a refrigerator, tables and chairs for meetings, a potter's wheel and kiln, an easel and racks for storing canvases?

• Does your activity require special lighting? If you work with harsh chemical substances or paints, do you need extra ventilation? Will the space house a rare book or art collection requiring separate climate-control systems and protective window shades?

• Can your work area be located behind doors? If you plan to have children and an office underneath the same roof, I would advise separation so that you can concentrate on each of them fully.

• Do you have people visit for meetings at home for which you need privacy, or can a room such as the dining room work for this purpose. Are there staff members or assistants who need their own work area?

• Describe how your ideal room might look. Think of environments in film scenes that have appealed to you: an American law office from 1940? A science lab? A New York loft space? A Tibetan temple? A Moroccan lair?

• What amenities do you want in the room? What is the one feature or furnishing you must have to truly make this your personal pleasure dome? A fireplace? A deck? French doors to a private garden? A wall of windows? An overstuffed sofa? A massive table to spread out your work? A terrific sound system? Indulge one fantasy if you can.

• If you like to exercise at home, or want to begin to, perhaps a gym and home spa is the room you want. If so, what type of exercise do you do? What equipment do you need: exercise machines (specify), weights, mats, hang bar? Do you need a large mirror to check your form, towel racks, a hamper, a refrigerator for water and juices? Does your ideal room include a TV, a stereo, a massage table, a shower, a sauna, or a hot tub? If your space or budget is limited, what are the items you simply cannot do without?

• Determine where you are going to keep your library. In the office? A reading room? The common room?

Utility and Storage Rooms

If we think of them at all, utility rooms and storage spaces are often the last we consider, relegated to some unused portion of the mind just as they are relegated to the attics and basements of our homes. Nevertheless, they deserve some attention since a well-planned utility space is like a well-greased cog in the machinery of life—it just makes things easier.

• Do you have enough storage in your home? Look for wasted spaces that can be turned into extra closets or storage areas.

• Have you planned for adequate electrical outlets and lighting in your home tool shop? Gas and plumbing hookups in the laundry room?

• Even the garage and attic need a lightbulb and switch. Have they been wired for electricity? Are they adequately insulated? Ventilated? Have you considered a powerful attic fan to cool the house on hot summer days?

• Do you know where the hot water heater is located in your home? The circuit breakers? The boiler? Electric and water meters? Make sure these utilities are accessible for easy servicing.

Exterior Spaces and Garden Rooms

I have already said much on the subject of gardens. Like nature itself, a garden is a work in progress, never the same from one day to the next.

• Think of your landscape as an extension of your home. What kind of outdoor rooms do you want: a child's play space, a patio to entertain, a meditation bower, an aromatherapy garden? Location is important. Be aware of fruit trees, particularly near dining or children's areas. They can be messy and attract insects.

• Garden rooms can take on their own distinctive look and feel, depending upon your preferences and tastes—perhaps a minimalist Zen motif of stone and rock; an herb garden, monochromatic and aromatic; lush and fragrant flower fields dense with color; or architectural planters on a sky-high terrace. Which suits you?

• Does your property offer the privacy you desire? There's much that can be done (plantings, screenings, fences) to enhance it. If you use containers for your plantings, know their characteristics: Do they absorb water? Must they be taken indoors in winter? Are they too large or heavy to be easily relocated?

• Do you wish to include structural elements such as stone walls, rock formations, walkways, terraces, sculptural elements, trellises? What about water features—a reflecting pond, waterfall, fountain? If positioned next to a window, the soothing water sounds will drift into your home's interior space.

• Notice possibilities for outdoor lighting, music, exterior electrical outlets.

• An outdoor grill and cooking station (permanent or portable) can be a wonderful addition.

• Begin to look at the many styles of outdoor furniture that are now available, old and new—tables, chairs, lounges, sun umbrellas, all in various materials. Do you have adequate storage for seasonal furniture as well as tools and garden supplies?

• What about your recycling and disposal needs? Have you

planned for a compost site and a convenient place to store unsightly garbage cans?

• Gardening can be wonderfully relaxing, but it is time consuming. Will you have a landscaper or gardener to do the maintenance, or do you plan to tackle it yourself? If you do it on your own, familiarize yourself with the practical aspects of the job. Trace the sun's path across your property in all seasons, and select plants that will thrive accordingly. Have your soil tested, and take steps to prepare it properly before planting. Know the relevant rules and regulations in your community regarding tree maintenance near utility lines, maximum fence heights, weight limitations for apartment terraces, and so forth.

• Access to water is essential to gardening. Is an automatic watering system a possibility? Are there regulations or restrictions in your community concerning their use? A convenient water outlet and hose connection are essential to water plants, rinse tools, and clean off muddy dogs and children.

Entertainment and Communications

Home entertainment and electronic communications have become such prominent and integral features of our lives that they warrant a separate place in this survey.

Nothing brings the family together like a good film on an outsize screen. Boxy TV sets have given way to HDTV transmissions viewed on slim profile monitors that hang on the wall like artwork. Audio and visual equipment, which once fit into a compact media center, now can fill a whole room and, in many homes, does. Our phones have memories longer than our lists of friends. Intelligent houses can be turned on and off by the flick of a remote button. And the once disparate functions performed by various electronic equipment—making phone calls to faraway friends, recording music, playing videos, making home movies, not to mention writing and sending mail—are all done by the home computer. Now even the homebound and disabled can shop without stepping out the door.

You may not have the space or desire to give over an entire room to your electronic toys, but you certainly will need to consider where you want to keep and enjoy them. This technology is constantly evolving, so your plans for this space must also consider not only what's available today but also what new developments will present themselves tomorrow. Keep it simple but be prepared. Give careful consideration before installing coaxial cable, speaker cable, phone jacks, computer ports (at desk height, please), and outlets for the continued electronics revolution. The Internet and e-mail are rapidly changing the way we communicate, but we still want our homes to have a comfortable place where we can communicate in the old-fashioned way—sitting together with friends over a cup of tea or glass of wine.

So revel in the new bounty of electronics. Invest carefully.

Learn to use these new toys and enjoy them, but keep the comfortable armchairs.

Audio

• Do you enjoy listening to music? What kind? How loud?

• Where are your favorite places for listening? Do you like to sit in one spot or listen on the move?

• Do you need more than one sound system in the house—and special soundproofing or other kinds of buffers—to accommodate the varying musical tastes in your home? Do you want concealed wiring? Built-in sound system housing is problematic. Keep it flexible for future upgrades and the possibility of obsolescence. Provide for ventilation of equipment.

• Are exterior speakers appropriate?

• How do you like to store your music: by type or alphabetically? How do you prefer to handle the differences in size among CDs, tapes, and albums? Do you allow cassettes and CDs to travel away from the main storage space? Does this cause conflict? Are you hanging on to old cassettes and disks that you do not listen to anymore?

• Do you own vehicles with sound systems? How do you handle the cassettes or CDs that you want in the vehicles and at home? Should there be one main collection that always stays in the house?

TV and VCR

• In which rooms do you like to watch television? Do you like to watch movies, and, if so, where's your favorite spot? Are TV and video viewing activities the family tends to do together or separately and alone?

• Do you want a TV within view where you exercise? In a workroom? The kitchen? A bathroom? Wherever you install a monitor, always position the screen away from unshaded windows to avoid glare.

• Would remote earphones be useful in your household to save family feuding over when, where, and what to watch? Earphones are ideal for any members who share a bedroom—or any room in the home—but not viewing habits.

• Where will you store videotapes and DVDs? Always store these items away from extremes of temperature and direct sunlight. If you like to record favorite shows or documentaries, are you hanging on to tapes that you do not use?

• Most people do not like exposed cable. Decide in advance what should be hidden so that the cable guy doesn't come in and staple a length of white cable across your red dining-room wall.

• Place floor-mounted electrical outlets flush to the wall, and for convenience locate control switches near the door.

Reading

• Where do you like to read? Have you installed proper lights there?

- Do you like to put your feet up while reading? Do you prefer a sofa or a chaise, or an armchair with an ottoman for better back support?

- Is your reading usually recreational or for study or both? Do you have a reading desk if you are doing research, or do you like to spread out the daily paper? Do you have a place close at hand to keep pens, notepaper, or scissors (for compulsive clippers of news articles or coupons)?

- Do you like to store books in various areas of the house: cookbooks in the kitchen, art books for browsing on a coffee table, dictionaries and reference books on your desk, novels in the bedroom? Or, do you want to consolidate your collection into a library? Incorporate a stepladder into your design so you can reach the high shelves.

- Do you wear reading glasses? Consider buying multiple pairs and keeping one in a decorative box or bowl nearby all the usual reading spots—bed, kitchen table, armchair—so you always know where to find them.

Communication

- Is there one spot in the house to find and leave messages, perhaps a chalkboard in the kitchen with clips on top for notices, cleaning receipts, and prescriptions? You could turn the entire kitchen door into a chalkboard by painting it with blackboard paint. In a child's room, a huge chalkboard or bulletin board allows for loving messages, reminders, and jokes.

- Is the telephone answering machine centrally located and accessible to all?

- Do you have an e-mail account? If not, think about signing up for one. It is inexpensive and swift and less invasive than a phone or fax.

- Which rooms need telephone jacks? Consider installing a phone jack in every room where you might use your computer and e-mail. Phone jacks are not technically difficult to install, but the cables leading to the jacks will often look like an oversight if they are put in after a design is complete.

- Does each person in the house need a mailbox stationed somewhere near the entry for incoming letters and magazines? Keep a wastebasket nearby so you can toss out junk mail instead of moving it from place to place or letting a big pile build up.

- Do you forget things at home when going out? If so, a bench by the front door is useful for leaving bags, letters to mail, and things to bring to the office, dry cleaner, or repair shop.

- Do you have a place for maintenance manuals with names, addresses, phone and fax numbers, and e-mail addresses for all immediate family?

- Are you prepared for your own death or disability? This is one area that most people do not think about practically. Keep a book with all your bank account numbers, your will, birth certificate, passport, and any private papers to which you may want your loved ones to have access—and *communicate* to them where you have stored them and how you want your affairs handled.

COLORING IN THE DETAILS

The final step in creating your wish list is to start coloring in your mental sketches by choosing your favorite textures, patterns, materials, finishings, and hues for each room.

This is also the time to start thinking about and preparing for the many practical details of your remodeling or decorating project, including any plans for construction, electrical and plumbing work, and other installations—and the related safety and maintenance concerns. Use the checklists that follow to help you keep track of all the particulars and record your final choices, as well as any personal remarks and pertinent data.

Textures and Materials

Carefully consider the textures of the materials that will surround you. You would not wear something made of a fabric that didn't feel good on your skin, so think about the tactile quality in addition to the look and durability of each piece of architecture and furniture in your home. Most people have some preexisting preferences in this realm, but be sure to examine all the options. Familiar materials used in unfamiliar ways can take on a completely new aspect. Be as lavish as you can. An expensive, high-quality material that will save money on maintenance costs might be cheaper in the long run.

Aim for a play of textures and materials. Sandblasted wood, stone, concrete plaster, slate, linen, and sisal are dry and matte. Glass, mirror, metal, high-gloss paint, and lacquer are sleek and wet. Chenille, velvet, area rugs, and carpets are opulent and warm, as are woods that are finished with oil, wax, or matte finishes.

For each category I've offered some of my own observations. Think about the rooms in your home and how these materials might work for you. If there are certain materials that would thrill you as flooring, but that you would never want in a table, make a note of that, too.

- **Wood.** The virtues of wood are numerous. It is warm and the grain is decorative. It can be stained to preserve the grain or painted almost any color. A long tradition of woodcraft spans almost every culture, and you can achieve a wide range of looks and levels of finish with this material. *If you like wood, which tone do you like generally: dark, medium, light, bleached? Grain or no grain? Finely carved shapes or big rustic chunks? Solid or veneer?*

- **Metal.** Think in terms of metals you have seen in nondomestic environments, such as black cast-iron, swirled-brushed steel, or rusted train rails. Stainless steel looks clean and slick and is reflective and durable. Bars of steel facing on concrete or plaster corners provide a linear element and a sense of solidity. *Do you prefer white- or yellow-toned metals, shiny or dull, rusted or patinated?*

• **Stone, slate, and brick.** The natural variations in these materials provide relief from the vastness of painted and man-made surfaces. Granite is the most hardwearing of common stones, and it behaves well in a kitchen. Sealed limestone, slate, and bluestone are warmer, and the slight staining these stones acquire with use turns to patina. The way a stone is finished changes its color and reflective properties. *Do you plan to incorporate stone, slate, or brick in walls, floors, countertops, staircases, or elsewhere in your home?* Visit a good stone yard or stone supply company to see and feel the various qualities of stone. *Do you prefer creamy marbles? Roman travertine in dusky gold or terra-cotta? Dark green or pale green? Limestone in taupe, ocher, or beige? Do you like a flamed finish, a natural cleft finish, or a honed or polished finish?*

• **Plastics.** Laminates, Plexiglas, and vinyl all belong to a group of man-made materials that wear well and are very useful in some circumstances. Lab tables are made from a compound that is incredibly strong and can resist extreme temperatures. Plastics are very malleable and can be made in any color and degree of transparency. On the downside, many plastics are harmful to the environment. Check to see if the one you are considering is made in a responsible way. *Is a high degree of durability and a reasonable price important to you?*

• **Glass.** Glass has many outstanding qualities. It can be transparent or translucent. If used in the right thickness, it is strong enough to be structural. Consider lining a shower with glass—no grout means easy cleaning. A glass tabletop (at least one-half-inch thick) can be glamorous, but remember you can see *everything* that goes on underneath—the dog gnawing a bone or a couple playing footsie. To counteract this, consider sandblasting the underside and finishing it with a special sealant. An etched-glass panel in a bathroom door lets the sunshine in without the loss of privacy. Clear glass room screens create interesting reflections and provide an unexpected sense of privacy by offering acoustical protection. A one-inch-thick tempered-glass floor in Felissimo, a department store I designed in New York City, is strong enough for fifteen or more people to dance on. If there is a possibility of impact, use tempered or laminated glass (always check this with your architect or engineer). Tempered glass will shatter into hundreds of little pieces; laminated glass hangs onto the coating material.

Sandblasting the edge of clear glass eliminates the green edge. A very white glass called Starfire Glass has no green edge. Glass comes in gorgeous colors reminiscent of stained-glass cathedral windows. A new and lovely innovation is the use of fabric, rice paper, or other materials sandwiched between two layers of clear glass—so easy to clean. We have used stainless-steel mesh sandwich for a door, translucent rice paper for a kitchen. I have used three-quarter-inch glass for a kitchen counter and have stacked it on a vanity top to make a diffuser for a light. Glass can scratch quite easily, but then so can steel and granite. *What type(s) of glass would you like to see in the new interiors?*

• **Plaster.** Timeless and resonant, plaster is a favorite material of mine for walls, showers, and floors. It dignifies a space or building. Its tough qualities give it the equivalent of a lifetime guarantee. The plaster still clinging to the walls in Pompeii is beautiful and sensual. A ding only enhances plaster finishes. It can be made in any color, troweled actively or serenely, made rough or smooth. When sealed, it will reject stains. You can swirl in metal dust or mica chips to reflect the light in an unpredictable way. *Are there surfaces in your home that would be good candidates for a plaster finish?*

• **Concrete.** This wonderful material with the visual weight of stone is suited to casting, troweling, or pouring. Concrete is obedient. I use it for tubs, sinks, and flower vases. I will pour a floor in an apartment and patina it with copper or bronze or aluminum. Concrete can be as smooth as satin or rough and pitted, and it wears well and looks good with age. Formulated correctly, it can be used outdoors as well as inside. There are special agents for coloring concrete in a range from mahogany brown to mint green. Like any natural material, there will be variations from batch to batch in the surface and the color. These variations are what we look for, so if you need more control over the surface, another material will suit you better. This is a versatile material, but it is almost guaranteed to get tiny fissure cracks. Make sure you will be able to celebrate and like this natural phenomenon rather than obsess about any flaws. *Can you use concrete in creative ways in any part of your design?*

• **Paint.** Paint is as versatile as you are. You can find textured paints, metal paints, and heat-resistant paints for radiators and light fixtures. Finishes range from mirrored gloss to velvety matte. The same color used for a wall in matte can be applied to the baseboards and moldings in satin to give a gentle play of interest. Note your choices in a binder that also holds the color chips and sources of the paints you use so that you can replicate them if an area needs to be repainted or touched up. *In what ways would you like to use the amazing array of paint colors and textures to establish a mood in particular rooms and closets?*

• **Fabric.** When choosing fabrics, think about texture before moving on to color. Fabrics can be lush, textured, slick, sheer, sturdy. Velvets are warm in the winter, but also in the summer. Prepare a foamcore board and use Velcro to attach samples of things you are considering. You can easily compare them and take them on and off as you narrow down your selection. *How hard do you need your fabric to wear? What kinds of fabrics would best suit the style of furniture that is going into your space?* The fabrics that come into contact with your skin, such

The Law of the Land

BEFORE YOU PURCHASE PROPERTY, KNOCK OUT A WALL, OR DIG THE FIRST HOLE IN THE GROUND, THERE ARE PRACTICAL CONSIDERATIONS THAT MUST BE ADDRESSED. THESE INCLUDE POSSIBLE PHYSICAL AND LEGAL LIMITATIONS ON WHAT YOU CAN DO AS WELL AS IMPORTANT ENVIRONMENTAL CONCERNS.

Orientation You can do many things to a piece of property, a house, or an apartment, but you can't change the course of the sun or the view. However, you may be able to edit a view by pruning or removing trees (if they belong to you) or even berming the earth.

Space Is the space you have right now enough for you? Is it possible to expand your home as your needs change? Consider an addition to the existing structure: adding outbuildings, acquiring an adjacent apartment, adding a mezzanine or a second story, or simply making the existing space work better for your needs through good design.

Weight Is there a limit to what the soil of your lot or the floor of your building can support? If so, how much effort and money will it take to correct it?

Structural Columns and bearing walls limit what can be moved or opened up. Cracks and settling are often indications of structural problems in existing buildings.

Environmental

• Water. Always check the potability of water, as well as its softness and mineral content. Make sure that there is an adequate supply – you wouldn't want to buy a house on a mountaintop and later find the cistern's rainwater is the only source of water.

• Drainage. Low-lying properties can have problems with heavy rain collecting, pooling, and running off from neighboring property, leading to a backed-up septic system, wet basement, or even flooding.

• Sewage disposal. Is a municipal system available, or will you need to provide a septic system? If so, establish that there is sufficient room and siting available for it.

• Plantings. Existing and potential trees and plants provide aesthetic value and shade and help to prevent soil erosion.

• Soil content and contamination. It is wise to research the former uses of a property and its neighbors so that you are certain you are not going to be living near unhealthy pollutants.

• Special environmental hazards. Familiarize yourself with the local history and pattern of severe weather and geological occurrences, including hurricanes, flooding, high winds, tornadoes, earthquakes, mudslides, and brush fires. You can take preventive steps to minimize the loss of property in a catastrophe by choosing the right construction design and materials, such as roof tiles instead of cedar roofing to protect against fires.

Playing by the rules Who has authority over the work you plan to do? A number of regulatory bodies may have a voice in the approval of your building plans, including co-op or condo boards and the local department of buildings, landmark commission, zoning board, review board, and others. Research the review and approval process. How long will each step take, and how much will the process cost? You may need to bring in an architect and/or an engineer to make your project happen. In some cases, you may even need a special consultant just to help you deal with the local bureaucracy. Typically, regulatory authority extends to:

• What you can build (zoning, deed restrictions, local appropriateness).

• Where you can build (required setbacks and restrictions for building within a lot).

• What you are allowed to change in an existing house or apartment and any special requirements, such as disabled access, landmarks, etc.

• Who can do the work. Apartment buildings and developments often require licensed contractors. They may have a preapproved list of contractors who can work on the premises or require that you hire only union labor. In any event, make sure your superintendent and building manager are included in the process and rewarded, as appropriate.

Environmental Checklist Unfortunately, our homes are not always the refuge we would like them to be. Environmental pollution has become the silent enemy, attacking us through extended exposure when we—and our children—are at our most vulnerable:

• Radon. Radon is the result of radioactivity from rocks, soil, or groundwater, and it can seep into the home and gardens through the foundation or tap water. If trapped in a tightly constructed house, radon levels can reach dangerous levels.

• Electromagnetic field pollution. Prolonged exposure can cause stress and hypersensitivity and may be carcinogenic, especially among children. High-voltage power lines are the primary cause, although household appliances such as a leaking microwave oven or television may be culprits as well.

• VOC (Volatile Organic Compounds). These toxic compounds are found in a number of common household products, including interior finishes, such as polyurethane, PVC in plastics, strong cleansers, and insecticides. They are noxious irritants at normal room temperatures and can generate highly dangerous fumes in a fire.

• Formaldehyde. This toxic chemical is used as a glue and preservative in plywood and particle board as well as in plastic products. Emissions cause skin and respiratory irritation and even cancer under normal temperatures, and like VOCs, potential hazards increase in the event of fire.

• Lead and cadmium. A well-known cause of brain damage, especially among the young, lead is found in old plumbing pipes and, along with cadmium, in old paints. For removal and disposal, contact authorized personnel.

• Dust. Up to forty pounds of dust accumulate in an average-size house every year. A mixture of organisms and dirt, dust can aggravate allergies or even carry disease. Installing traditional and electronic filters in HVAC systems and maintaining those filters on a regular basis is one way to reduce the problem.

• Mold. Mold is any of various types of fungus. It grows in damp areas within walls and ducts as well as in basements and can trigger allergies and carry infectious diseases.

• Asbestos. This construction material was widely used until the mid-70s and may be present in insulation, fireproofing, radiator enclosures, and floor and ceiling tiles. Airborne asbestos particles are especially dangerous and should be removed and disposed of by authorized personnel only.

• Combustion hydrocarbons. Gas boilers and gas kitchen ranges, especially in poorly ventilated areas, can pollute a house with carbon monoxide, carbon dioxide, and nitrogen dioxide; an improperly vented fireplace or heating stove in an enclosed space can lead to dangerous carbon monoxide levels.

What to do if you have a problem To determine and solve a problem with any of these household pollutants, consult with an expert. Local authorities often provide testing for established pollutants like asbestos, lead, and perhaps radon. For information about newer threats, contact: Environmental Construction Outfitters at 718-292-0626 or Environmental Home Center at 206-682-7332.

as furniture upholstery, should be tactile and pleasing. *What tactile qualities do you prefer against your skin?*

Color

Color plays a vital role in establishing the mood of a room, as well as in broadcasting your taste. Dark colors make a large room snug; light colors lift your mood. A room painted in an intense color, like deep red or a lush orange, makes your heart beat faster when you walk into it. Color is contextual. The same shade of gray can look like a bruise in a brown-toned room or a stone in a white room. You may hate a red tie but remember a wonderful red dining room that you loved.

• Start to think about colors that you enjoy or would like to see in your surroundings—colors that make you happy or calm or draw you in for some reason. Refer to the color sections throughout the book if you need a place to begin. Do you prefer golden, late-afternoon colors by the beach? The aged reds and flax colors of Pompeii? The freshness of blues and whites with the silver-green of olive trees in Greece? Close your eyes and run the video that we all have in our minds of places we have loved. Pay particular attention to the colors that make up that landscape. Make notes of the mood each color triggers in you and the pleasant nostalgia it calls up.

• Go through your home, room by room, noting your favorite colors. Are the colors you prefer in the abstract best suited for walls, floors, and ceilings or for objects or pieces of furniture? Also note the colors you dislike—colors that jolt you, irritate you, or make you conscious of them.

• Try to find samples for each color you desire to have in your home so that there is no misinterpretation later on. Samples can be pages torn out of magazines, pieces of fabric, or stone or wood—anything that helps to guide your thoughts toward fulfilling what you really want. Clippings from fashion, food, and travel magazines often help define a good sense of color and mood.

Safety and Maintenance

Electrical and lighting. Electricity can kill. If you are installing or moving outlets or switches, consult an electrician about local codes and the available amps in your space. If you are building a home, the mechanical engineer or electrician will calculate this for you based on the number of appliances and the amount of lighting you require. Always use a licensed electrician to ensure that installation is up to standard.

• Plan out the placement of outlets for phone, electricity, Internet, and cable to eliminate the visual clutter of cords stretching across the room. Note on your checklists the lighting, appliances, and electronics that need to plug into a wall, and consider the furniture around them so that you can place outlets for easy access.

• How many lamps do you need in each room? Where will you place them? Note where you will need ceiling lights, track lights, wall lights, attic or ceiling fans, and any other permanently placed electrical fixtures.

• Do you prefer low light, focused light along walls, or general light that comes from above? Lighting types often work best in combinations. Downlighting tends to compress energy and uplighting enhances it, so use both types to find a good balance. Visit as many lighting showrooms as you can to research the types of lighting you like; the salespeople are generally knowledgeable. Refer to page 72 for additional ideas.

• Use surge protectors for your sensitive electronics.

Security, Privacy, and Safety

• How many locks do you need on your doors? Do you need a peephole for your entry doors? A chain? A video-intercom? If your building has no doorman or security, do you need an alarm system or a hotline to the police station programmed into your phone?

• Do you want to be able to turn off your doorbell?

• Do you want an unlisted phone line for outgoing calls, with a second line hitched onto a message machine so that you can easily screen all your calls? The phone is a mixed blessing, and unwanted callers can intrude at the wrong time.

• Which interior doors, cabinets, or storage areas in your home or office should ideally have a lock? Who will have the key?

• If you have children, do you have a secure place (either out of their reach or secured with a lock) to keep medications, over-the-counter drugs, and potentially harmful household products? Do you have safety bars on all windows?

• Do you have private papers or valuables that you want locked away between uses? If so, do you want to build in secret storage or purchase a safe? Does the safe place have to be fireproof?

• Do you have an escape role in case of fire? Where do you plan to locate your smoke alarms? Is there a sprinkler system, or can you install one? Have fire extinguishers in your home, and ask your local fire department to show you the best places to keep them.

• Do you have photographs, receipts, or other identification papers related to artwork, expensive furnishings, and other valuables as necessary for your insurance coverage? Are these records stored in a fireproof box in your home, or will they be stored in a bank vault?

Energy Conservation and Environmental Concerns

• Take full advantage of available light and air. Is there a place to locate a skylight? Skylights lend great energy to a space and are often less expensive to buy and install than you think.

• Take advantage of energy audits and the implementation of their findings for cost-saving bonuses and tax deductions.

• Do not forget about the benefits of insulation, double-glazed windows, solar panels, and ceiling fans, which can all work to make your space warmer in winter, cooler in summer, and generally more pleasant to live in throughout the year.

• Thoroughly investigate your heating, cooling, and cooking systems to make sure that air exchange is rapid and that environmentally sound fuels are used. Install humidifiers and air filters or ionizers if you have allergies. In a new construction, it is best to have these built in.

• Join your architect or designer or landscaper in the search for nontoxic paints, varnishes, and sealers; nonthreatened woods; materials that do not release gasses after installation; and indigenous plants and natural weed and pest control for your garden or terrace.

• Have you allowed space for recycling containers? Each year more things become recyclable. For now, allow for paper, plastic, cans, glass, and bottles in addition to refuse that cannot currently be recycled, such as food scraps and diapers.

• Investigate nontoxic, biodegradable cleaning agents such as bleaches, dishwasher powder, and polishes for use in your new space.

Tax Considerations

• Have you consulted with your accountant or tax adviser as to how best to use and declare your renovation or building investment to obtain appropriate deductions and benefits? These might apply at the completion of renovation, during your use of the space, or, in the case of ownership, at the time of resale.

• A certificate of capital improvement may be available so that you do not have to pay sales tax on your installations until the completion of resale.

• Do you work at home? If so, I recommend that you look into every possible deduction and available benefit from the IRS.

FINALIZING YOUR WISH LIST

The left side of the brain has done its analytical work, and now it's time to let your imagination soar. Use this short list of questions to trigger recollections of childhood fantasies and all the things you have ever wished for in your dream house. Go within and touch your own deepest personal desires and nostalgia. This is the moment to decide your top priority—the focal point of your home design. These are the decisions you will live with, happily or not, for many years to come.

• What are the "must haves" for your space, the rooms or elements without which you will never feel truly expansive and happy in your home? A fireplace, a pool, a mahogany-paneled study, a sun room with wall-to-wall windows, a screened-in porch, a cavernous basement workshop, a skylit marble bathroom with floor space enough to dance, a terraced garden, a billowy canopied bed, a built-in aquarium?

• Do you dream of a home boutique, a room just for your clothes and accessories, with a packing table and suitcase storage, all on view and carefully coordinated? Perhaps a toilet and bidet *en suite*? A Jacuzzi with a garden view? Thick carpeting, plush seating, and floor-length mirrors everywhere?

• Is it time to indulge your collector's instinct? Do you want glass-fronted cabinets to display Limoges, or built-in shelves for rare books? At last you can have a place to show and share your treasures.

• Do you want to knock out walls to make one communal room where TV, music, communications, cooking, conversation, food, and games all take place? If you are feeling boxed in by life, this could be the breakout change that really makes a difference.

• A workout room is high on many people's list. Is yours fully equipped with the latest exercise machines and a spa with Jacuzzi and sauna—so you never have to leave home? How about an indoor pool with a hallway right off the master bath?

• Is food your passion? Do you want a wet bar and a wine cellar? A dining area that you can set like a stage, with every beautiful prop hand chosen and placed in the perfect spot? Do you dream of having a kitchen with every professional appliance and gadget, every electronic convenience, endless counter space and storage, and suspended above it all a cable-ready TV tuned to Food Network?

• Perhaps your ultimate self-indulgence would be a space dedicated to romance and sensuality. Imagine a small retreat with a waterfall, comfortable seating, floor cushions, candles, and gentle lighting, a still place where you and yours can go to meditate, converse, listen to music, or make love.

• Have you always nurtured a secret talent or harbored a passion that you could finally unleash if you only had your very own space to do it? Sculpting, painting, writing, weaving, potting, cooking, reading, sewing—the list is endless. Now is the time to experiment fearlessly. Joy and growth are in the doing. Realize the dream!

USING YOUR WISH LIST

By now you should have a far better sense of how you and those you share your home with will be using the space, and what configurations, materials, and other special features will enhance your lives there. Use this information to inform your conversations with architects and designers, and to guide you as you work with contractors, vendors, and other suppliers for your home. I hope that *Total Design* can direct you and those who help you realize your dream home toward an environment that is a uniquely satisfying place for you to inhabit.

Resources

FOR A COMPLETE LISTING OF THE RESOURCES, STORES, AND ARTISANS WHOSE WORK AND PRODUCTS APPEAR IN THIS BOOK, PLEASE LOOK ON OUR WEB SITE: WWW.CLODAGH.COM. MANY OF THE PRODUCTS SHOWN ARE ALSO AVAILABLE DIRECTLY FROM THE CLODAGH COLLECTION, 670 BROADWAY, NEW YORK, NY 10012, 212-780-5300 (FAX: 212-780-5755).

ALTERNATIVE MUSIC
Peter O'Kennedy
22 Cameron Square
Kilmainham
Dublin 8, Ireland
011-353-1-454-5699

APPLIED ARTISTS
Architectural Sculpture Associates, Inc.
Multimedia
Alan Swanson
740 West Vine Street
Lancaster, PA 17603
717-393-4688

Espen Eiborg
Fine Artist
338 Berry Street
5th Floor
Brooklyn, NY 11201
www.eiborg.com

Get Real Surfaces
37 West 20th Street
New York, NY 10011
212-414-1620

Harris Rubin
Metal, Wood
84 Front Street
Brooklyn, NY 11201
718-858-6165

Henry Royer
Metal, Wood
110 North Thornton Ave.
Building C
Madison, WI 53703
608-257-2102

Robert Younger
Concrete
274 Water Street
New York, NY 10038
212-233-8251

Square Deal Construction & Design
Custom Fabricator
Jeff Ford
238 North Ninth Street
4th Floor
Brooklyn, NY 11211
800-493-9161
718-218-9113

Terence Main & Kim Kuzmenko
Functional Fine Art
423 Grand Street
Brooklyn, NY 11211
718-384-0105

Tony Conway
Metal, Multimedia
519 West 26th Street
New York, NY 10001
212-564-3262

BATH
Ann Sacks
5 East 16th Street
New York, NY 10003
212-463-8400

CARPET
Lees Carpets
(Licensee)
3330 West Friendly Avenue
Greensboro, NC 27410
800-523-7888

DRAPERY
DFB Sales, Inc.
21-07 Borden Avenue
Long Island City, NY 11101
718-729-8310

ENVIRONMENTALLY FRIENDLY PRODUCTS FOR HOME/OFFICE
Harmony/Seventh Generation
360 Interlocken Blvd, Suite 300
Bloomfield, NJ 80021
800-869-3446

EUROPEAN STYLE
Design Yard
12 East Essex Street
Dublin, Ireland
353-1-67-78453

Kilkenny Design Centre
Castle Yard
Kilkenny, Ireland
353-56-22118

FABRICS
Avora™ FR by KoSa
4501 Charlotte Park Drive
Charlotte, NC 28217-1979
704-586-7525
www.avora.com

Coraggio
979 Third Avenue
New York, NY 10022
212-758-9885

Design Tex
(Licensee)
200 Varick Street
8th Floor
New York, NY 10014
800-221-1540

Cowtan & Tout & Larsen
979 Third Avenue
New York, NY 10022
212-753-4488

FENG SHUI
Sarah Rossbach
(All inquiries through Clodagh Design International)
670 Broadway
New York, NY 10013
212-780-5300

FLOORING
Amtico
Linoleum, Conseal
200 Lexington Avenue
Suite 809
New York, NY 10016
212-545-1127

Metaphor Bronze Tileworks
(Licensee)
Jay Gibson
P.O. Box 397
Ringoes, NJ 08551
908-237-9570

New York Flooring, Inc.
Wood Floors
129 East 124th
New York, NY 10035
212-427-6262

Stone Source
215 Park Avenue South
Suite 700
New York, NY 10003
212-979-6400

FOUNTAINS
Modern Stone Age
54 Greene Street
New York, NY 10013
212-219-0383

FURNITURE & ACCESSORIES
Dennis Miller Associates
(Licensee)
306 East 61st Street
New York, NY 10021
212-355-4550

Felissimo
10 West 56th Street
New York, NY 10019
212-247-5656

Holly Hunt
979 Third Avenue
Suite 605
New York, NY 10022
212-755-6555

Niall Smith Antiques
344 Bleeker Street
New York, NY 10014
212-255-0660

Tucker Robbins
366 West 15th Street
5th Floor
New York, NY 10011
212-366-4427
www.tuckerrobbins.com

GLASS
Duncan Laurie
P.O. Box 78
No. 2 Ft. Wetherill Road
Jamestown, RI 02835
401-423-3992

John Degnan
415 Lafayette
New York, NY 10003
212-420-7887

HOME ACCESSORIES
Muse
(Licensee)
Linens, Candles
One Design Center Place
Suite 444
Boston, MA 02210
617-330-7891

Terra Verde
Environmental Home Furnishings Store
120 Wooster Street
New York, NY 10012
212-925-4533

INTERIOR DESIGNER REFERRAL SERVICE
Designer Previews
Karen Fisher, President
36 Gramercy Park East
New York, NY 10003
212-777-2966

LANDSCAPE DESIGNER
Janice Parker
52 Wakeman Hill Road
Sherman, CT 06784
860-350-4497

Mark Yarris
428 Bute Road
Uniontown, PA 15401
724-439-5533

Miguel Pons
433 West 24th Street
Apartment 1F
New York, NY 10011
212-255-6310

LIGHTING
Boyd Lighting
(Licensee)
944 Folsom Street
San Francisco, CA 94107
415-778-4300

Ingo Maurer
89 Grand Street
New York, NY 10013
212-965-8817

Lightforms
169 Eighth Avenue
New York, NY 10011
212-255-4664

MARKETING CONSULTANT
Tim O'Kennedy
17 New Wharf Road
London, England NI 9RB
011 44 171 713 5474

UPHOLSTERY
De Angelis Upholstery
312 East 95th Street
2nd Floor
New York, NY 10128
212-348-8825

Furniture Masters
81 Apollo Street
Brooklyn, NY 11222
718-599-0771

Jonas Upholstery
44 West 18th Street
10th Floor
New York, NY 10011
212-691-2777

Linda Fryling
57 North 6th Street
Brooklyn, NY 11211
718-388-0162

WALLCOVERING
Vescom
Vinyl Wallcovering
245 Wescott Drive
P.O. Box 1201
Rahway, NY 07065
732-382-7120

WALL FINISHES
Art in Construction
(Licensee)
Artisan Plaster
34 West 22nd Street
New York, NY 10010
212-352-3019

Loye & Derrickson
572 Plutarch Road
Highland, NY 12528
845-255-4211

Serpentine Studios
296 Elizabeth Street
No. 1F
New York, NY 10012
212-674-7235

222

Index

223